DENNIS VAN DER MEER'S
COMPLETE BOOK OF
TENNIS

DENNIS VAN DER MEER'S
COMPLETE BOOK OF
TENNIS

by
*Dennis
Van der
Meer*

A
tennis
MAGAZINE
BOOK

Published by Golf Digest/Tennis Inc.
A New York Times Company,
495 Westport Avenue
P.O. Box 5350
Norwalk, Connecticut 06856

Trade book distribution by
Simon and Schuster
A Division of Gulf + Western Industries, Inc.
New York, New York 10020

ISBN: 0-914178-56-3
Library of Congress: 82-80144
Manufactured in the
United States of America

Book design by Irene Friedman
Jacket design by Dorothy Geiser
Printing and binding by R.R. Donnelley & Sons

"Dennis Van der Meer is the best tennis teacher in the world." *– Billie Jean King*

Dedication

To all my students, from Wimbledon champions to those who are happy just to clear the net.

Thank you for making my life as a teacher so enjoyable.

— DVdM

Acknowledgments

No tennis pro develops a tennis teaching system or model like mine without the help of others. Many fellow professionals and players over the past twenty-five years have played a part in the development of my methods. Some who have directly influenced me are Billie Jean King, Tom Stow, Jaroslav Houba, Jim Verdieck, Jim Loehr, Stanley Plagenhoef, and Norm Fisher. Many hundreds of others have contributed, perhaps unknowingly.

To all, I am grateful. A special acknowledgment to Dr. Louie Cap, who has been my assistant for over ten years and who can read my mind on the tennis court, giving me exactly the right kind of shot at the right time when I give a demonstration. Louie, many thanks.

I also wish to acknowledge the assistance given me by Caroline Campaigne in the conception, writing and design of this manual.

CONTENTS

Introduction

Throughout my career, I've had the pleasure of teaching some of the world's best players and also the dubious pleasure of teaching some of the world's worst players. I know beyond a doubt that no matter what your playing level is, if you want to improve, my teaching method will ensure improvement.

In essence, my method can be reduced to a three-word premise: SIMPLE IS BEST. I often prove this point by starting a lesson hitting easy groundstrokes to my student with instructions to volley the ball from the net back to me ten times without a mistake. Usually, beginners can do this exercise quite easily. It is the exception, though, for an intermediate or even a relatively advanced player to keep the ball going. The player either hits the ball into the net or overhits the ball way out of the court. After watching the student struggle for a short while, I ask him to sit on a chair and repeat the same exercise. Suddenly, to the player's amazement, keeping the ball in play becomes very easy. By sitting on the chair the student simply reduces the number of moving body parts, thereby reducing the chances of error.

In later phases, I teach each stroke in parts, building from these parts to create a complete stroke. At the end of one week of instruction, even the least athletic beginners have a fair set of sound, basic tennis skills from which they can build a better game.

My method is based on sound biomechanical principles. In recent years, several recognized experts in anatomy, education and cinemaphotography have examined my methods using high-speed movie photography and computer science. These experts have found that my method of scientifically teaching tennis in progressive steps, from simple to complex, is valid. Equally significant is that these same experts have confirmed my belief that many concepts still commonly taught, such as the wrist snap over the ball on the serve, the covering of the racket face over the ball for topspin in groundstrokes, and the weight transfer from back foot to front foot during the hit, are biomechanically unsound.

I have taught my method to more than four thousand teaching professionals throughout the world and at my Van der Meer Tennis Center at Hilton Head Island in South Carolina. It has become recognized worldwide as the Standard Method™ of tennis instruction. Tennis pros who use this method are certified by the Professional Tennis Registry of the U.S.A., and you can be assured of receiving sound, basic instruction from USPTR members throughout the world. There are of course many other competent tennis pros who use individual teaching techniques that are quite compatible with my method.

Over the years I have taught, directly or indirectly, several million children and adults to play tennis. The most difficult aspect of teaching adults to play tennis is to convince them that they most certainly can improve and correct faulty techniques. Moving into the thirties or forties, some players believe that they are irreparably set in their ways. They seem convinced that trying to improve their tennis is senseless because their physical abilities, most notably quickness of foot and eye, are starting to decline. Nothing could be further from the truth. Any loss of physical ability can be countered by improvement in stroke technique and tactics.

The late starter should never envy those who started playing as youngsters. The fact is that even extraordinary players like Bjorn Borg and Tracy Austin can only look forward to playing worse tennis as they get older, whereas those who begin tennis later in life can always expect to improve.

A word for the young player too. Young players have the advantage of speed of foot, strength of leg, suppleness of body and quickness of reflex. But good technique and biomechanically sound, basic strokes are as indispensable to the young player as to the adult player. Tennis has become a tremendously competitive game, and if an aspiring champion has an obvious flaw or shortcoming in his stroke production, you can be sure his opponents will take full advantage of it.

One final point. This book will serve you well as a textbook, but you should also have regular checkups on your stroking techniques by planning lessons with your own professional. Using this book in conjunction with lessons from a pro who uses the official Standard Tennis Method™ will greatly facilitate your instruction and improvement.

Good luck and may all your first serves go in!

PART I

The Serve

The Forehand

THE BASICS

The Backhand

The Volley

Serve

1.

For beginners, the serve starts the point. For good players, the serve opens doors—to put-away volleys and untouchable overheads.

Naturally, every tennis player wants to be good and no one admits to being a neophyte. (That is why self-rating systems don't always work!) And, I would wager that every tennis player believes that the essence of being good is to serve the unreturnable ace.

The result is that everyone tries to serve that dream serve. The only snag is, the blasted thing rarely goes in. Now what do you do? You weakly dink the second serve into the court and get ready to run down your opponent's return.

One would think that tennis players would learn from these horrible experiences. Not so. Logic apparently has nothing to do with tennis. A fellow at my former club in Berkeley has missed approximately one million first serves, but he is sustained by the memory of his one big cannonball serve that went in in 1942 (or was it 1943), when he aced Bill Tilden.

Not only is this so senseless, but this perennial tactic actually dooms many a player to mediocrity for life. Why? Because a neophyte who starts off hitting the ball hard is using strength instead of developing the flexibility and elasticity of a good server. And once he has learned to use only his strength, no matter how long he plays, he will never have that smooth, beautifully coordinated serve of the champion.

Conversely, once a novice is resolved to serve properly, I can teach him in about one short hour to swing smoothly and hitch-free.

STROKE PRODUCTION

I have developed a variety of teaching exercises helpful in developing and perfecting the elements of a classic serve, devoid of all quirks, frills, jiggles, and squiggles. These exercises are valuable to players at all levels. For the beginner, they develop a smooth serve. For the player with a hitch, they ensure a continuous rhythm. For the good player, these exercises reemphasize basic sound movement and help eliminate unnecessary flourishes.

The Stance

The service stance is simple and something that every person has done hundreds of times without knowing it.

Serve: Stance

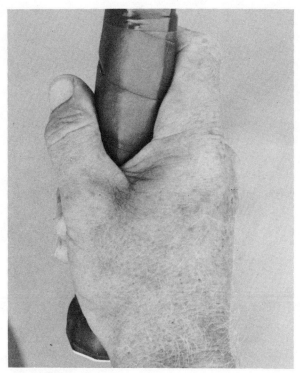

Serve: Grip

Have you ever waited for a bus? You surely then know the service stance. Ever been to a cocktail party, a bit semibored and listening patiently to someone holding forth endlessly on some triviality? Well, congratulations! You know the service stance. It is simply a stance which places most of your weight on your back foot, your feet about shoulder-width apart, and your front foot turned outward about halfway. That's it. That is all you have to know about the service stance. Forget about the famous Newcombe rock from front to back foot. Forget about the weird John McEnroe knee twist and the little hoppity-hop of Vitas Gerulaitis. Neither will add a thing to your game.

The Grip *(also see Chapter 19)*

Raise your racket fully extended toward the sky, with the edge pointing toward the net. The hold that feels most natural will be the service grip. (It will probably be halfway between a forehand and a backhand grip.)

THE CORRECT SERVICE GRIP

In the old days we told students to use the forehand grip on the serve, and only after they had become more experienced could they use the correct service grip.

The reason was that most tennis teachers believed that there was a wrist snap over the ball and inexperienced players just could not get the hang of the serve. (The only people who could learn to serve were kids—because they ignored our advice and learned correctly despite the instruction.)

Several years ago I did some research on the biomechanics of the serves of Arthur Ashe, Ken Rosewall, and John Newcombe. By using slow-motion film, I could plainly see that there is no wrist snap over the ball, but that the racket turns from right to left as the forearm pronates.

To learn pronation, merely extend your arm toward the sky and let the edge of your racket point toward the point of contact. *Now* turn your forearm so that the face of the racket is facing the intended point of contact. This is the key move. From here you can build the serve by:

1. Dropping your racket behind your back and reaching up to the ball while turning the forearm.
2. Adding a follow-through.
3. Swinging the racket down and back instead of lifting it up.
4. Combining the rhythm of the backswing and the toss.

Today nearly anyone can learn a smooth serve with the correct service grip.

Throughout these service routines, *don't change this grip!* Now you and I will go through the whole routine from here.

The purpose: this simple exercise demonstrates the wrist turn for the correct contact point and also the correct weight-shift pattern.

Point of Contact and Back Tapping

Again stand ready to serve with the racket head behind your back. This time toss a ball up, reach up exactly as you did in the previous exercise, with your weight shifting forward, and tap the ball, but do not follow through. Stop at the point of contact.

Serve exercise: Drop racket behind your back. Reach up with the racket edge pointed toward the net.

BUILDING THE SERVE

Contact Point and Weight Shift

First, from the serving stance, drop the racket head behind your back, then reach straight up to the sky with the racket *edge* pointing toward the net. Simultaneously transfer your weight from your back foot to your front foot with only the toes of your back foot on the ground.

Second, repeat the exercise, but this time reach toward the sky with the racket *face* of your racket toward the net.

Serve exercise: Drop racket behind your back. Reach up with the racket face pointed toward the net. This movement of the wrist demonstrates correct pronation.

Serve exercise: Drop the racket behind your back. Reach up with the racket and release the ball. Tap the ball and stop at the contact point with your weight forward and arm fully extended to establish your correct contact point for the serve.

The purpose: to identify the correct contact point, demonstrate proper weight transfer, and establish a correct ball toss to the contact point. By freezing at the tap, you can check to be sure that your weight is forward, and your racket arm is fully extended.

Karate and Follow-Through

Again start in the serving stance with the racket head behind your back, reach up and tap the ball gently, but this time follow through slowly to a count of ten until the racket head has completed its full arc. It is in the slow and deliberate follow-through pattern that you will see the wrist turning from right to left after ball contact in a karate-type motion.

Repeat slowly.

The purpose is to groove the point of contact and exaggerate the follow-through. You are training your muscles. Repeat the exercise slowly and carefully to ensure its correctness.

Down Together and Up Together

Every move till now has been very easy, but now you have to coordinate the left arm with the right arm. Follow this sequence exactly.

Take the service stance, simultaneously swing the racket down and touch your back with the racket while reaching up with the ball hand. Start again. This time swing the racket head back and touch your back while you release and catch the ball. The first few times it will feel almost as though you were being told to rub your stomach and pat your head, but you will quickly get the hang of it.

Now comes a tricky part. Swing the racket back and touch your back *twice* while releasing and catching the ball.

Finally, from the serving stance, swing back, touching your back twice while releasing the ball, and this time hit the ball gently and follow through.

Repeat, touching your back only once.

> **MYTH:** Snap your wrist over the ball for a more powerful serve.
> *DON'T BREAK YOUR WRIST OVER THE BALL. ROTATE YOUR WRIST AND FOREARM FORWARD AND YOU WILL HAVE THE CORRECT SERVING MOTION.*

Now keep serving slowly, and gradually try to keep the racket swing continuous. Not holding your racket too tightly will greatly help you get the flow of the racket.

The purpose of this final sequence of exercises establishes the correct, uninterrupted and coordinated movement you want in your serve.

I suppose that I can now tell you why you had to touch your back twice. It was actually just a trick to let you know how much time you really

Serve exercise: After you have met the ball at the contact point, follow through slowly and deliberately.

Serve exercise: Take the service stance. Swing the racket down and touch your back while reaching up with the ball hand in a ''down together-up together'' motion.

have to complete the backswing. Most inexperienced players are fearful that they don't have enough time to complete the backswing, but this exercise allays all those fears.

The Ball Toss

At this stage I should also tell you something about the ball toss. I have deliberately not talked about it because I do not want you to become paranoid about how to toss a tennis ball two feet into the air. Nevertheless, with so many tennis pros driving Ferraris and Mercedes Benzes because they are instructing players in the special art of the tennis ball toss, I must tell you about the $42,000 tennis lesson. It is definitely an indispensable part of your tennis instruction and knowledge. Imagine this typical scenario.

''I can't toss the ball up straight,'' laments the hapless student.

''Pay me $42,000 and I will teach you how to toss accurately.''

''Expensive, but it is worth it,'' sighs the student.

Surely it is worth it, because the toss is the most difficult thing in the world. Why else would every tennis magazine have at least forty articles on the intricacies of the toss? Why else would your friends tell you how difficult it is? And how could tennis pros own big cars if it weren't for the money they received for teaching the toss?

How did all this come about? After all, you never had trouble at school pitching pennies during recess. And you gentler souls certainly remember tossing a beach ball all of five feet with credible accuracy. And now. . .you can't loft a tennis ball two feet into the air?

How, I repeat, did all this come about? Because at your first lesson, coordinating the ball toss with the backswing probably went something like this:

"Okay, now remember, as you swing your racket back, at the same time you raise your left arm and release the ball which you are holding lightly between your first and second finger and thumb. As you are about to release the ball, be sure that your arm is fully extended and that your racket has swung back down and is all the way down behind your back. Remember too that you have to shift your weight to the front foot as you release the ball. And, most important, don't ever hit a bad toss because you will catch an incurable disease if you do. Get it?"

You think you have everything straight, but somehow the whole thing reminds you of the Bud Abbott and Lou Costello skit "Who's on First?"

The one thing, the foremost impression you have been left with is. . .*never hit a bad ball toss*. So you put it all together. You fake, stall, jiggle, hesitate—yes, no, yes, no, now, later. . .*now!* And when you finally release the ball it ends up in the backstop behind you.

"I guess you will have to take the $42,000 ball-tossing lesson," remarks the ever observant pro. "The problem is, you are not holding the ball properly. You have two pounds of thumb pressure on the ball instead of one and a half pounds. Also, your index finger is crooked twenty-seven degrees instead of twenty-four degrees.

"Also," the pro continues, "the first thing you have to know is exactly where to toss the ball. You appear to be about five feet eight inches

tall. Let's see. . .approximate arm length is thirty inches and your racket length is about thirty inches less the grip. Hmmm. . . Well, okay. That figures the toss should be 118 inches off the ground, give or take a half inch. Also, the northerly direction of the ball, that is, toward the net, should be eighteen inches in front of your left foot and the westerly direction should be seven inches to the right of your nose because you have a regular-size nose. Otherwise we would have to make that six and a half inches. Now a very good way to know that you are tossing the ball correctly to that nebulous spot in the sky is to place your racket on the ground. Oh, yes, on the ground, right in front of you, and an accurate toss will land right in the middle of the racket face. Now go and practice the toss 500 times a day until next week."

So you practice diligently and you can now toss the ball and make it bounce right on that racket face in front of you every time. Who cares how high it might be going in the sky now!

Time for your next lesson, a week later. You are confident. After all, you can toss the ball into the air and have it land on the racket face on the ground every time.

You go through your checklist of instructions with the pro and then. . .here goes!

"Racket back. Ball up. Together now!"

And the blasted ball lands once again in the backstop behind you. But at least this time you did remember not to hit at it.

"Well, I told you it was not going to be easy. It will take many ball-tossing lessons and maybe by the time you have spent $42,000 you will have it!"

But, it really is not that difficult.

I start most of my Tennis University courses for pros with a demonstration of the serve. When the time comes to show the ball toss, I send one of my assistants out to scour the club for an attendant, a caretaker, or a bookkeeper, anyone who is not a tennis player.

Standing about four feet away from my "guinea pig," I ask him or her to toss a ball to the racket I am holding waist-high. This presents no problem. Then I move my racket higher with each successive toss until finally I am holding my racket fully extended above the guinea pig's head at the correct contact point for the serve. My guinea pig unerringly will toss the ball to the exact spot, utterly amazed that this seemingly simple act should be so wildly applauded by all the pros present.

I have done this little act several hundred times in my life. I have had guinea pig tossers of every age, shape, and size. I have never had one who could not toss the ball straight into the air.

What is the explanation? The problem with the service toss is not the toss. The problem is your divided attention as you swing your racket back and move your tossing arm forward. Anxiety develops because you fear you can't handle the two motions simultaneously.

Relax. Follow the simple sequences that I have outlined and you will have no trouble coordinating the toss and the swing.

What's more, *Always hit a bad service toss when you are practicing,* or at least complete the sequence of your stroke. By completing the entire service motion, you will each time visually identify where the ball should have been, the correct contact point and spot for the toss. Don't move your stance to chase the ball. Just follow through with your stroke. You will clearly see whether the ball is too low, too far in front, left, behind, or right. Use this information to keep adjusting the direction of your toss until you have zeroed in on the exact contact point with the racket.

I guarantee you no pressure, no anxiety. And it won't cost you $42,000.

Keep practicing the service motion. Start by standing very close to the net. Keep hitting very lightly and look for continuity in the swing. Gradually, step back a few steps at a time until you are finally serving from the baseline and the stroking pattern has become well established. Keep serving gently and work to develop a smooth serving rhythm. At first just get the ball in the court, then direct the ball from side to side.

Next add depth and gradually a bit more speed.

In the beginning, keep the motion simple. Don't step in with your right foot. Just concentrate on developing the correct service rhythm. Gradually, everything will start to feel more free and easy.

At this point you can start customizing your serve. You can add your own ritual before you serve the ball. Or you can imitate the way Jimmy Connors bounces the ball ten times or the way he tucks in his shirt. Perhaps you would like to blow on your hand the way Bjorn Borg does. Or rock back and forth like John Newcombe. Or grunt like Chris Evert Lloyd. Or cuss like Ile Nastase.

Seriously, though, at this stage you should start to step in behind your serve and follow the serve to the net.

It is also at this stage that you should definitely add variety to your serve by learning the slice and spin serve.

TYPES OF SERVE

The Slice Serve

The sequence for learning the slice serve is as follows:

First, visualize a clock face. Now this is probably easy for many of you, For those of you who have grown up on digital watches and can't relate to a clock face, go to a railroad station and look at one.

Be that as it may, stand between the net and baseline. Imagine the ball is a clock face. Choke your racket close to the throat, and gently bypass the ball with a movement of the racket, going from left to right to three o'clock on the ball. At this point, don't follow through, just make a short brushing move. (It will be easier if you use more of a backhand grip.)

The next step is to add a follow-through. This is a quite difficult step to understand because the racket starts off with the outside edge leading, and after contact the racket face turns over and your thumb side starts to turn in first until the

Position of racket face on ball for serve.
Flat   *Slice*   *Spin*

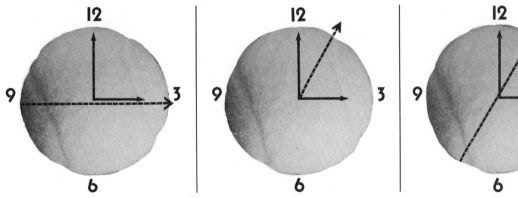
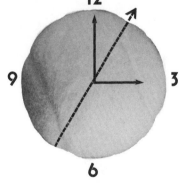

Serve: For a slice serve,
think the racket face brushes
across the ball to
"three o'clock."

Serve: For a spin serve,
think the racket brushes
across the ball at one o'clock.

Serve: For a twist serve,
think the racket brushes from
seven o'clock all the way
up to and over one o'clock.

Serve: Slice serve viewed from the front. Note the traveling path of the racket face.

racket face finishes turned inside out against the left knee. Now add a backswing, a down together rhythm, and you have an instant slice serve. Gradually, grip the racket closer to the leather grip and move back to the baseline.

By the way, your ball toss should be a little more toward the righthand side, but don't exaggerate too much or you will be telegraphing your opponent that you are going to serve a slice.

The Spin Serve

Once you have mastered the slice serve, you are ready for the big time.

Every decent tennis player must have a spin serve. Visualize one o'clock on the ball. As in the other serves, start off standing very close to the net. Choke up on your racket and brush by the ball; the racket should travel from left to right by one o'clock. Now add a backswing and a follow-through—the racket will swing from left to right and then finish to the left. The toss should be a little to the left, but again don't make it

obvious. Start off by practicing close to the net. Then move back slowly to the baseline.

The spin serve is an indispensable weapon in both singles and doubles. It does all the right things. You can hit the ball high over the net and still have the ball arc down into the service court because of the topspin. Apart from this margin of safety, some other benefits accrue. With a spin serve, you have more time to get to the net because the ball is traveling more slowly through the air. Another big advantage is the spin serve's high rebound. Many players have difficulty returning a high bouncing ball, particularly on the backhand side.

The American Twist Serve

If you want the ball to bounce even higher and have more of a kick toward a righthander's backhand, you can get more spin by brushing your racket from seven o'clock all the way up to and over one o'clock. This serve will give your ball a wickedly high bounce. The full American twist is quite strenuous on the back and is little used by tournament players.

PROBLEMS AND CORRECTIVE TECHNIQUES

As I have told you, anyone can go through the steps to learn or relearn the serve in a relatively foolproof manner. But invariably someone mucks up and needs a quick suggestion for a stubborn problem. In my lifetime as a teacher, I have seen every possible way to ruin the serve, so I have had to use many corrective techniques. Pick the one that describes your problem best and I hope it will correct your serve.

When you find that you have incorrectly become used to hitting your serve with a forehand or a Western grip, just place your racket under your

25

Serve: Spin serve from front.

arm like a British officer's swagger stick. Reach out and grab the handle. You are likely to have the right grip.

Some players are very tricky. They actually change their grip during the hit. If you make this mistake, cure it by pressing a dime against the handle of your racket with your index finger or thumb. If you then shift your grip, the dime will drop onto the ground.

Don't ever start the serve with your racket face toward the net. That is a sure sign of an incorrect grip. Turn the racket so that the edge of your racket points toward the net. This action will help to correct your grip.

Your stance should be natural. Nonetheless, some of you will insist on standing in a weird way. Those of you who are members of the National Rifle Association should imagine that you are lined up to fire a rifle. That should fix your stance immediately.

A quick nervous release of the ball during the toss produces a jerky motion and many bad tosses. To correct this, make a fist and rest the ball on your curled first finger and thumb just like a scoop of ice cream in a cone. Gradually, you may let the ball fit deeper into your hand as your toss becomes less jerky.

Sometimes you can correct your errors by doing the opposite. If you are a player who stumbled forward because your toss is going too far in front, stop this problem by walking backward at the moment of contact. Unconsciously, you will move your ball toss back to the correct contact point. After a few practices, you can begin to step in again.

In addition to tossing the ball too far in front, you might pick up the habit of tossing with a circular motion. Your ball hand travels back with the racket hand. This problem is easy to correct. Just practice your serve by standing close to a fence or wall so that your ball has to be released in front of your body.

Occasionally when serving you may believe that there is not enough time to complete a full backswing and still have time to meet the ball. Try swinging your racket back and touching your back twice before you hit the ball. You will have to rush like crazy. But now when you touch but once, you will have time for a cup of tea before hitting the ball.

The best way for you to find out where to toss the ball is to hold your racket at the spot where you would like to meet the ball and then toss the ball to that point.

Mis-hitting the ball is everyone's problem at one time or another. Especially on windy days you may find that your mis-hits increase. The cure is to keep your head up and your eyes raised until at least the point of contact, and you will find your mis-hits greatly reduced.

If you are having difficulty completing your serve on the correct side of your body, practice an exaggerated follow-through. Carry your racket through the stroke around your side and then actually clamp your racket with your left arm against your armpit at completion.

The day will come when you find that your serve is just "out of sync." You are tossing the ball too soon or too late. When your toss is too late, begin your serve by crossing your left hand over the right so that your left hand must go at the same speed as your racket. When your toss is too early, cross your left hand under your racket.

Of all the serving errors I see, the most common is a lack of continuity of the racket. Many persons get stuck somewhere along the line. A trick that usually cures needs the help of a partner. Practice your service swing without a ball. You will find this easy to do with perfect continuity.

Now have your practice partner toss a ball just as you start your downward swing. Without your having to worry about the rhythm of the

27

Serve. American twist serve from front. It is very similar to the spin serve. Ball is placed a little further to the left. And there is a little more arching of the back.

racket swing and ball toss, it is easy to keep the racket moving. Once you have had a few successes, toss the ball yourself. Should your hitch reappear, again have your partner toss awhile. Then try again. Gradually your hitch will disappear. A small reminder for the ball tosser: stand on the righthand side of a righthanded server and on the left for a lefthander. (That sounds like gratuitous advice, but you wouldn't believe some of the dumb things I have seen people do.)

SUMMARY

The serve starts the point and then becomes a formidable weapon as control and speed grow. With your mind's eye on a clock face, meet the ball at three o'clock for a slice, at one o'clock for a spin, at the seven to one range for an American twist, and at center where the hands meet on the clock face for a flat serve.

Don't let all these time references confuse you. A lady from Charlottesville, Virginia, wrote me, saying, ''Thank you for teaching me that the slice is hit at three o'clock and the spin serve is hit at one o'clock. It was most informative. Unfortunately, I can't use these serves because our foursome only plays in the mornings.''

Serve: One way to find the correct service grip is to grab your racket from under your arm like a British officer's swagger stick.

Serve: To discover where to toss your ball for the best contact spot, hold your racket up to the contact point and toss the ball to it.

Serve: The correct service stance can be duplicated by lining up to fire a rifle.

Serve: To ensure a smooth ball toss when serving, practice by releasing the ball from the top of your curled first finger and thumb.

Serve: To correct a circular motion in your ball toss, practice your serve and ball release while standing near a fence or wall so the ball has to be released in front of your body.

Serve: To ensure a complete follow-through, practice swinging your racket completely through and around to your side and actually holding the racket against the leg and tucking the racket under your arm at the end of the stroke.

Forehand

2.

When your opponent serves the ball, you must return the ball. And the word is *return* the ball—not *slug* or *kill* the ball. Simply *return*.

Once you return the ball, you must keep a rally going. So you need a forehand drive for returning the serve or for rallying.

One of the problems with the forehand drive is that players have a misconception about what the correct stroke should look like. There are great players, world class players, whose techniques seem markedly different from that which I suggest you use.

However, to hit the ball properly, you should start with the racket low and finish with the racket high. During the stroke from low to high, keep the racket on edge. With the racket on edge, the ball is propelled forward. The upward movement of the racket from low to high will impart topspin when the racket starts moving faster.

A comparison with good players unfortunately falls down here because many experienced players look as though they are covering the ball. Covering the ball means that the racket face is turned toward the ground at the moment of impact. Actually, they are not covering the ball. They start off closing the racket face, but at the point of contact the racket face flattens out. Then on the follow-through the racket face turns toward the ground again. The timing for this kind of shot is critical.

If you follow the concept of starting low, finishing high, and keeping the racket on edge, you have a little more leeway to make a successful shot, even if you are a fraction too early or too late. This is why I say keep the racket on edge.

Tactical misunderstandings are responsible for many biomechanical problems on the forehand. Understand your tactics first. One: Get the ball back in play. Keep a rally going. Two: Aim the ball from side to side. Three: Hit the ball deep to give yourself more time to recover and make your opponent's return more difficult. Four: Play aggressively by increasing the pace of your stroke and adding spin.

I know that most everyone goes for number four first. This tendency is further encouraged by racket ads that say, "Buy the XR-7-42-zz. Our racket is the greatest racket in the world because it will hit the ball faster than a speeding bullet."

I know no tennis player who cannot already hit the ball hard enough and out of the court.

What I am waiting for is this kind of ad: "Buy our racket. It doesn't hit the ball very hard, but it hits every ball right on the line!" That is the racket I want to buy.

Be sensible about your tactics. I'm not suggesting you go through life pushing and pooping the ball into play. Take a chance once in a while, even when it's risky. And when you have a fairly good chance of success, take a whack at the ball! But overall, temper your pace with some logic and do not club every ball.

STROKE PRODUCTION

We will now go through a series of steps that will help you develop a sound, classically flawless forehand drive. If you are a beginner, you will learn the movement without any problem. If you are an intermediate player who has developed some peculiarities, you will quickly become aware of them as you go through the various stages. And for advanced players, the steps should remind you how important proper preparation and positioning are for stroking the ball.

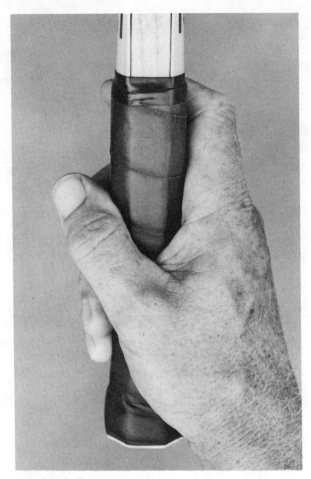

Forehand: Grip

The Grip (also see Chapter 19)

You will enjoy your tennis more if you have a grip that enables you to hit the ball in a sound manner. I have seen many players start with a grip—an extreme Western grip or a Continental grip—they have lived to regret. Once you learn one grip it is difficult to unlearn it. So take the trouble *now*, if you are not a long-time tennis player, to learn to hold the racket properly.

What would be correct? There are many slight variations in grips, but what you are really looking for is one that enables you to have most of your hand behind your racket. If you find that, you will be able to learn a classically sound forehand quickly.

An old but tried and true approach to find the correct grip is to shake hands with the racket. If you can shake hands with your racket while the racket is on edge, you will have the correct grip.

Another clue. Your thumb and first finger should form a *V* on the middle of the racket grip—if you are over thirty. Kids don't have *V*'s, they have *U*'s. You have a *V* because the web between your thumb and index finger has become a little distended.

> **MYTH:** *KEEP YOUR RACKET ABOVE YOUR WRIST.*
> Don't. Just maintain the angle between your racket and forearm throughout the stroke. Under these conditions your racket head will be above the wrist on some shots and below the wrist on low ones.

Forehand: Stance

The Stance

Now that you have the grip, what is the ready stance for the forehand? It is not a big deal. Your feet should be comfortably apart. Be in a position where you are alert and expecting to respond to your opponent's stroke. Lean slightly forward, your back should not be rigidly straight.

Don't bend too far over. Stand in a comfortable position. Put your weight on the balls of your feet, not on your toes. If you put your weight on your toes, you are likely to fall over. The left hand supports the racket. Remember, tennis is a two-handed game to that extent. The left hand and right hand act together to give you balance.

STEPS TO THE FOREHAND DRIVE

Turn Your Shoulders

Your first move! The opponent serves the ball. You respond. *The first thing you must do is turn your shoulders sideways*. As you turn your shoulders sideways, you also move your racket. Your shoulders turn and racket moves as a unit. As you turn, your racket turns with you.

The turn may vary. You can either pivot, simply meaning you turn on your right foot, or take a step with your right foot to the right side. Or if the ball is close to your body, you can pivot turn by stepping away with your right foot behind your left foot. Or if the ball is in front of you, you can start to make the pivot turn by stepping with your right foot in front of your left foot. As long as you make the pivot and shoulder turn, everything else will follow.

Racket Back and Down

You are holding your racket in front of you

Forehand: Shoulder turn

in the waiting position, but after you make your turn your racket will be pointing to the right sideline. You will see that your racket head is too high. The ball is going to bounce to a height somewhere between your knees and your waist—but your racket head is almost shoulder-high.

So *move your racket backward and lower your arm*. Then your racket will be parallel to the ground. The butt of your racket will be pointing straight toward your opponent.

This becomes quite easy with practice. Say to yourself, ''Turn, racket back and down,'' as you go through the motion.

Adjust Your Feet

Step forward on your left foot and transfer your weight forward to the front foot.

Forehand: Racket back and now to get the racket head below the height of the ball, lower your arm.

ideally, your racket hand should finish opposite your left eye. That is the forehand drive movement.

Let's do it again.

- You have the grip.
- You have the stance.
- Now turn your shoulders.
- Take your racket back and down.
- Step onto your front foot.
- Swing to the point of contact.
- Follow through.

Now let's go through it one more time, but this time let us add one more tricky segment, which is essential.

- Grip.

Contact

Swing forward. Swing to the spot where your arm feels comfortable and strong. This contact spot most likely will be a little in front of your left leg. Keep the racket head on edge throughout the swing. Depending upon your grip, the contact spot varies. If your grip is somewhat like a Western grip, the spot will be more in front and the racket face will tend to be closed. If your grip is Continental, the spot will be further back and the racket face will be more open.

Follow-through

From the contact point, keep swinging forward. Move your racket hand forward and gradually upward. Finish with your racket opposite your left eye. Actually, not your racket, but,

Forehand: Adjust your feet to place your weight on your front foot at the moment you begin your forward swing.

Forehand: Careful follow through

- Stance.
- Shoulder turn.
- Racket back and down.
- Now this time don't step forward with your left foot. Instead, *run a few little*

steps. Just a few little steps toward the net. Stop with your left foot in front. In other words, you now have the same position as you had before when you just took the one step.

- Now swing and follow through, finishing with your racket hand as high as your left eye.

That is all there is to the forehand. Talk yourself through it. Grip—stance—shoulder turn—racket back and down—adjust feet—transfer weight to front foot—swing through to point of contact—follow through.

STROKE DEVELOPMENT EXERCISES

Now that you know the fundamentals of a classic forehand stroke, let's practice the stroke with a live ball. Here is a good routine for grooving your forehand stroke production.

Contact Point Exercise

Go to the point of contact and hold your racket at the point of contact. Have your practice

Forehand—Steps to the Forehand Drive: 1. Stance and shoulder turn • 2. Racket back • 3. Adjust your feet and weight before contact • 4. and 5. Complete follow-through

partner toss you the ball. You do nothing except move your racket from the contact point all the way through to the follow-through. *Hold* the follow-through so that you and your partner can see whether you are in the correct position. Repeat a few times.

Complete Stroke Exercise

Take your racket back and hold your racket so that the butt of the racket points toward your partner. At this stage, add a few adjusting steps to run toward the net. Stop. Now have your prac-

tice partner toss you the ball. Slowly and gently swing straight forward to meet the ball with your racket gradually rising until your racket hand is as high as your left eye. Repeat a few more times.

Do both of these exercises close to the net. Stand about four or five yards apart from your partner.

Backswing—Hit—Follow-through Exercise

This time face the net. Turn. Take your racket back and down. Have your partner toss you the

Forehand exercise: Trap the ball at contact several times to establish the optimum contact point.

Forehand exercise: After you have hit the ball, hold your follow through to groove the stroke pattern.

ball. At the same time, run with a few adjusting steps and stop. As the ball arrives, swing at it. Follow through completely, so that your racket hand finishes opposite your left eye. Do this exercise several times.

CHECKPOINTS

Your index finger should be a bit extended when you have the grip. Don't clutch your fingers too closely together.

As for your stance, be sure that your left hand is supporting the racket properly. Remember, your knees are to be a little flexed and relaxed, not rigid.

When you make the shoulder turn, be 'sure your weight is transferred to your righthand side.

As you take your racket back and down, *don't change the angle of the racket*. Don't drop the racket head down. Yet don't keep it artificially high. Try to keep the angle the same throughout.

After you take some small adjusting steps and finally put your *weight on the front foot,* again be sure that your front knee is relaxed and not stiff.

While swinging to the contact point, remember to *swing from your shoulder*. You will feel your hip relax a little, allowing your shoulder to come through.

On the follow-through, emphasize *low to high*. If you remember to keep the racket perpendicular or on edge, you will hit the ball forward. Keep the follow-through high and finish with your racket hand opposite your left eye.

At the completion of the stroke, stand still for two or three beats. Analyze what you have done. See whether you have turned forward. Are your hips and shoulders facing the net? Is your racket arm fully extended and is your weight on the left foot? The toes of your right foot should just touch the ground. This is a good picture of the end of a sound forehand drive.

Working slowly, you will find the entire routine for learning the forehand drive takes approximately thirty minutes. If learning the forehand can be so simple, why are there so many weird-looking forehand drives?

The reason is that though the basic mechanics of stroking the ball are simple, *ball judgment* plays an important role in proper stroke execution. Judging the approaching ball creates the problems.

How quickly can you see whether the ball will come to your forehand or not? How quickly can you get your racket back? How quickly can you adjust your feet to make the point of contact exactly at the right spot? How well can you follow through in a perfectly balanced manner?

That is the challenge. Your degree of success in these areas will determine how well you eventually play your forehand drive.

At this stage of learning, some players invite trouble by hitting too fast and without control. You begin using a makeshift technique to return the ball. If you are late in preparing, you fall backward, meet the ball behind your body, and use no follow-through.

After a few hits like that, this bastardized stroke begins to feel okay. You continue to fall back, hit the ball, and use no follow-through! You end up scooping the ball and it seems to work.

Unfortunately, the more you use this improper stroke, the more it becomes ingrained.

My suggestion is this. While you are learning to play properly, play mostly *under control*. Match your ability to that of your opponent so that you can grow step by step.

Your game will grow sensibly and soundly if your partner across the net also follows the correct tactics and techniques. Start your practice sessions slowly with the ball moving at an easy speed.

First groove your stroke. Then you can play a faster ball. The ball will start arriving faster, but you will be able to respond more quickly. You will be able to make the adjustments because you are building your skill step by step.

While practicing, have your partner toss or hit you some high bouncing balls so that you quickly have to adjust your feet to get into the right position.

Have your practice partner hit or toss the ball

right in front of you so that you can practice stepping away from the ball.

Also have your partner toss or hit you deep shots so that you will quickly have to run backward, stop, and then step in again.

These are the stroke patterns that you are going to have to use when you play matches. Start practicing now so that you will know every way the ball can bounce.

PRACTICE DRILLS

Once you know the correct technique you can begin to practice, but you cannot rally yet. You don't have the rhythm of the game yet. You must develop rhythm with the ball going back and forth across the net.

Here is a drill to help you develop this rhythm. Stand across the net from your practice partner with your racket touching your partner's racket. Back away from the net three or four yards. Very gently tap the ball back and forth, without any backswing and with only a slight follow-through.

Beginners will find this drill easy. Intermediates will suffer a bit. Advanced players had better watch out because they will probably find this little drill difficult. They are not used to playing easy shots. The drills, however, will be useful to advanced players because they will be forced to recognize the different rhythms and speeds of the ball.

As you develop control during this drill, move back a few steps at a time. Always keep the ball in play. Gradually back up to the service line. Practice your rally from the service line and then move back a little more. Make a game of working your way all the way to the baseline and perhaps beyond and then work the rally toward the net again.

While you do this drill, familiarize yourself with all the different lengths of the court. You will see how hard you have to hit the ball from different distances and still keep the ball in the court.

As you move back, your backswing gets longer and your follow-through gets longer.

Forehand: Forehand slice

Gradually you will develop ball control and ball sense.

Eventually, you marry your ball sense to the correct stroke. Once the two are equal in skill, you will begin to understand what a forehand drive is. Your whole movement will become fluid and continuous from the initial response, shoulder turn, racket back and down, adjusting steps, weight going to the front foot, racket meeting the ball dead center, and follow-through. All this will be one smooth movement.

Now you can really play the forehand drive.

THE SLICE

You can slice the ball, rather than come up

on your groundstrokes, by changing the face of your racket from perpendicular to open, and by changing the pattern of your stroke from "low to high" to hitting through the ball with a glancing blow.

Slice imparts an underspin to the ball which causes the ball to stay in the air longer. A sliced ball should give you more time to prepare for your next shot, so it is also a convenient defensive weapon.

Follow the stroke production pattern detailed for the regular forehand stroke, but add two variations. First, instead of maintaining a perpendicular racket face throughout the entire stroke, keep your racket face open, slightly tilted toward the sky throughout the entire stroke, from the racket back position through the follow-through.

Second, after you turn your shoulders in preparation for the stroke, take your racket back without lowering your arm. Your grip will be the same, but the racket face will be opened a bit. The stroking pattern of your racket will be racket back, and then you will hit through the ball at the same level as the backswing.

PROBLEMS AND CORRECTIVE TECHNIQUES

Now that you know the perfect stroke, what can possibly go wrong? Plenty.

One thing that can go wrong is that Dan, the football player, will forget that he is playing tennis and think he is still on the gridiron. The football coach at Dan's high school said, "Always face your opponent." So Dan juts out his chin, faces the net, and attacks the ball. He has to learn to get his shoulders sideways for a proper stroke.

Your problem may be like housewife Nellie's. She thinks that the racket is a dishcloth, so she slaps away at the ball. Wrist control is essential for a controlled stroke.

Barry the butcher slices meat with neat little chops. Since Barry plays tennis on his days off, he should learn how to play a drive as well.

There are many other stroke problems and peculiarities for which I would like to suggest some cures. Pick the suggestions that best suit your problems and see if they help.

A proper grip is important. If you want to change your bad grip, your problem will be that your new grip will gradually slip back to your old one. Try this little trick. Hold a pen in writing

Forehand: Correct a wandering elbow by tucking a tennis ball underneath your arm and holding it there until you swing. The ball should not drop out before contact.

position while you are gripping the racket. When you are rallying, the angle of the pen will tell you whether you are reverting to your old grip.

Another problem is leading with your elbow on the backswing. Sometimes experienced players intentionally lead with their elbows to develop more leverage. These experts take their elbows back to give the racket an extra bit of momentum and power. This is a very tricky action to accomplish though. Most people end up in trouble trying to duplicate this elbow-lead movement.

If you find that your elbow is going too far from your body at the beginning of the stroke, tuck a tennis ball underneath your arm. Hold the ball under your arm as you turn and take your racket back. Only when you follow through should you see the ball dropping out. Should the ball drop out before you complete your backswing, you will know that your elbow is jutting out too much. This is an excellent exercise to encourage you to use a compact backswing.

Mis-hits are bad for your soul, bad for your tennis, and bad for your tennis elbow. Often a student will ask me whether the size of his grip makes his racket twist in his hand. No. Mis-hitting makes the racket twist in the hand.

When you hit the ball off center, the racket will twist in your hand. To alleviate this problem and help you find the "sweet" spot, play catch. Toss the ball up in the air, let it bounce on the ground, then trap the ball with your racket and your left hand. Do the exercise with a partner on the other side of the net.

By practicing this exercise, you will understand how important positioning and footwork are to sound hitting. After a few sessions, you will find that you try to watch the ball meet the racket and mis-hit the ball less frequently because of your improved positioning.

When you discover that you are using too much wrist on the forehand, concentrate for a while on moving your arm back and forth, instead of the racket.

If this does not correct your wrist motion, actually tape your wrist with masking tape for a practice session so that the wrist action will be

Forehand: Don't stare too long at the ground after contact. You'll forget to turn your shoulders into the stroke.

reduced and you can regroove your stroke motion.

Sometimes even the best forehand is marred when a player loses his balance during the stroke. To solve this problem, hold your finish for a definite one-two-three count during a practice session so that your footwork and body position will be perfect for you to hold steady throughout the entire stroke action.

Another common forehand flaw is slapping at the ball, essentially rushing the last phase of the stroke. Rebuild your timing to correct this error by starting your shoulder turn the minute you anticipate your opponent's return is going to your forehand court. Then carefully time your

Forehand: Simple "straight back" forehand stroke production.

forehand as you move through the stroke so that each part, the turn, racket back, adjusting feet, stroke and followthrough, is unrushed and unhurried.

By the way, don't try to correct mis-hits by staring at the contact point long after the hit. This won't help your stroke production.

Unfortunately, this has become something of a rage as a corrective technique and I will tell you the reason. A few years ago Billie Jean King was having trouble with her backhand approach shot down the line. She was moving her head and opening her hips too quickly. As a result, the ball was sliding off her racket. She was repeatedly hitting the ball wide. In an attempt to trick her to keep her head still and stay sideways through the stroke, I had suggested as a temporary correction that she look backward as she hit the ball. On the sidelines, someone saw her do this and assumed, "Oh, boy! This is a revolutionary way of sighting the ball better."

In short order, this new "technique" was printed in magazines and even experienced pros started to use BJK's new trick! Any ophthamologist will tell you that from an optical point of view the idea is bad. Furthermore, from a biomechanical standpoint this idea is horrible. The free flow of your shoulders and hips is affected. Furthermore, the player must dip his shoulder to an extreme, which further hinders the swing.

Of course, if you are a coin or bug collector, this technique may help you spot something for your collection. But it won't help your forehand one iota.

A CONTINUOUS SWING

The simplest way to take your racket back is merely to turn your shoulders. Your racket itself does not really move, but turns incidentally with your shoulders. Then you use your arm to get your racket back.

As your tennis ability grows, try to develop a continuous backswing that will be somewhat circular and more efficient. You will observe that the circular backswing, a high accelerating swing with fast deceleration, is prevalent among the current crop of tennis stars. Some of these players lead their backswings with their elbows to produce extra whip and speed on the return. As they lead back with their elbows, the face of their rackets closes somewhat on the backswing, but flattens out again just at contact with the ball.

Inexperienced players observe this racket action and incorrectly surmise that the pros are hitting the ball while closing over the ball with the racket face, and are thus producing topspin.

This simply is not true. Even the pros meet the ball with their racket faces straight on. Their timing, though, is so precise that the racket face actually travels a pattern of being closed on the fast backswing, meeting the ball straight on, and then seemingly closing again as the pro completes his extended and exaggerated follow-through.

As you play more often, your elbow may start to rise and you will get more acceleration out of the more circular movement.

However, be careful that you do not become a high accelerator and decelerator with limited success. Rather, be a consistent player, playing the game by moving your racket back a bit more slowly. You may lack velocity, but you will have more accuracy.

To add 5 mph to the speed of a tennis ball requires a tremendous amount of energy. Why not direct the ball a foot or two further away from your opponent?

Until you are sure of your ability to produce the super topspin, use the simpler and more controllable technique of turning your shoulders with your elbow tucked in close to your body.

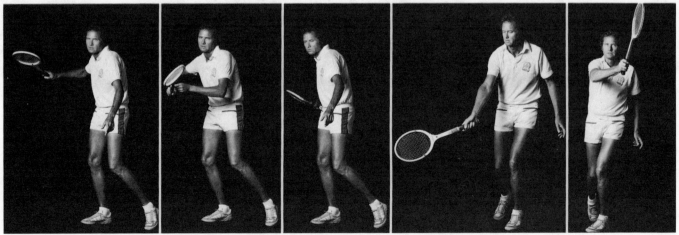

Forehand: Advanced forehand with a raised elbow which closes the racket face on the backswing of the stroke.

Backhand

3.

The backhand is difficult. There, I have said it. The backhand is difficult.

True, every experienced player and club pro will say: "Oh, the backhand is so easy! You will have no difficulty learning the backhand. The backhand is biomechanically simpler than the forehand!"

And yet, you and I both know very well that the backhand is difficult. For several reasons. One is that we are not used to swinging from the backhand side. It is different.

A second reason is that the successful backhand is dependent upon the correct grip and the strength of the forearm muscles. Whenever you look at the forearm of an experienced player, you will see substantial muscle development right at the elbow where the forearm starts. These are the extensor muscles, and the reason they are so well developed on the experienced player is that he has hit many backhands. Unless you have well-developed extensor muscles, you will find the backhand difficult.

The good news is that once you start getting the feel for a backhand, once you become familiar with the grip, and once you start swinging from your shoulder, the backhand stroke becomes simple and a real pleasure.

Happily the sequence of the execution of a proper backhand stroke is similar to that of the forehand. You get the proper backhand grip, turn your shoulders, drop your racket back by lowering your arm, adjust your feet to get into position, hit the ball from low to high, and complete your follow-through.

The backhand differs from the forehand execution mainly in the grip, which places the hand more on top of the racket and creates a sharper angle between the racket and your forearm.

Another difference is that the shoulder and hip rotation in the backhand is more curtailed because the ball is hit almost entirely from the shoulder. In the forehand your shoulders and hips usually finish facing the net. The backhand stroke finishes with your hips having made only a quarter turn forward. Because of the limited hip turn, the backhand is hit with a closed stance most of the time.

Learning a sound basically flat backhand is essential for a good level of play. As you become more experienced and the racket head starts to accelerate, this relatively flat drive becomes a topspin drive.

STROKE PRODUCTION

The Grip (also see Chapter 19)

For the correct Eastern backhand grip, turn your hand a quarter turn toward your body. Extend your index finger slightly to firm up your grip. Your thumb may be either slanted down across the handle or curled under it.

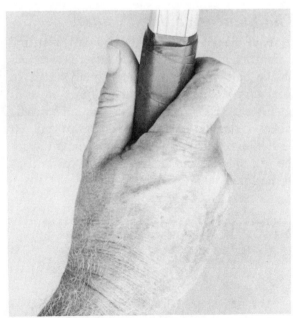

Backhand: Grip

you will automatically transfer your weight to your left foot. Still keep your racket on edge and don't change from your backhand grip. Bring your racket down by lowering your arm. You may want to touch your thumb to your thigh as a guide to lowering your racket far enough.

Backhand: Stance with the backhand-grip

MYTH: *TRANSFER YOUR WEIGHT FROM YOUR BACK FOOT TO YOUR FRONT AS YOU HIT THE BALL.*
No. Your weight should be transferred before you hit the ball. Power comes from hip and shoulder rotation.

The Stance-Waiting Position

Face the net with your knees slightly bent and weight evenly distributed, slightly forward and on the balls of your feet. Hold your racket in front of your body. Keep your elbows close to your sides. Use your left hand to support the racket. Using the correct backhand grip, you will be holding your racket so that it points toward the left sideline rather than straight forward as in the forehand.

STEPS TO THE BACKHAND DRIVE

Turn

The first step of the backhand movement is to turn your shoulders. Pivot to your left so that

Backhand: Turn

Adjusting Steps

Step toward the net with little steps to reach the best hitting position. Shift your weight to your front foot before hitting.

Point of Contact

Hit the ball in front of your right leg, at approximately thigh level. Keep your arm relatively straight at contact.

Backhand: Adjust your position and shift your weight forward

Backhand: Racket down

Note that the angle between your forearm and your racket remains relatively the same throughout the stroke. Because of the backhand grip, this angle will be greater than on the forehand.

Follow-through

Make your follow-through a long, continuous sweeping motion, from low to high. *Use your shoulders. Don't straight-arm the shot.*

During the stroke, rotate your hips and shoulders a quarter turn toward the net. At completion of the stroke, your arm should be quite extended with the racket head high.

SPECIAL BACKHAND PROBLEM: THE GRIP CHANGE

Of the problems that you will encounter on the backhand side, the most pervasive among all tennis players who learn as adults is the grip change. It is not the backhand grip itself that is difficult to learn. I can give you numerous illustrations of what the actual grip looks like. The problem is *remembering to use the grip*.

Another problem for players who are learning to make the grip change is that many very good players do not make obvious or substantial changes from the forehand to the backhand and these players quite often unintentionally influence beginners and intermediates not to change their grips. I must admit that if you learn to play

tennis as a youngster, it is possible to make adjustments, develop strength, and learn to play backhand strokes very well without substantial grip changes. But youngsters have a lot of time to learn these things.

My suggestion is that if you want to learn to play the backhand more quickly and with success, you must concentrate on making a substantial grip change. And once you have the grip change and know how it feels, then you have to practice switching your grip from forehand to backhand quickly. It is no good being able to play a backhand without being able to return the next ball that comes to your forehand. Practice how to make the grip change from side to side.

And also remember, don't change the grip midway through the swing. *Keep the same grip throughout the stroke*.

Backhand: Hit and follow through

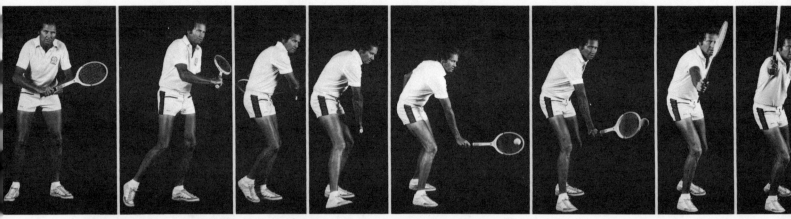

Backhand: Stance • Turn • Racket down • Adjust position and weight forward

Backhand: To find the proper backhand grip, break your wrist and point your racket toward the sideline, turn your hand until the wrist is pointing toward the sky.

Now, how do you find the grip? What are some clues? I have various suggestions. Here is an easy and direct method. Just hold the racket straight out in front of your body. Point the racket straight toward the net. Now break your wrist and point the racket toward the sideline. You will see a lump where the wrist is broken. Turn your hand toward your body until the lump is gone. Now you will see that your wrist is pointing toward the sky. You are putting a lot of support and strength behind the racket with the meaty part of your palm below the thumb.

Here is another way to find the backhand grip easily. Hold your racket against your left side with your left hand so that the racket shaft touches your left hip. Now reach over and put your right hand on top of your racket. Again, try to put the fatty part of your palm behind the racket. You

kissed by a Frenchman. Raise your hand up in that limp back-of-the-hand kissing position. Then close your hand firmly on the racket and you have the backhand grip.

A fourth trick for learning the backhand grip is to choke up on your racket. Hold your racket

Backhand: Choke up on the racket to get the feel of the right backhand grip. Then slide your hand down the shaft while keeping the same grip.

Backhand: To find the correct backhand grip, hold your racket on your hips, reach over and put your hand on top of your racket.

can extend or curl your thumb around the racket, whichever is more comfortable.

Another method for getting the right backhand grip is to imagine that your hand is being

halfway up the shaft. By doing so you will easily feel the grip with your knuckles on top and the support from your thumb. Now slide your hand back and hold your racket full length.

One final clue to make your backhand feel more comfortable. Extend your index finger a bit on your racket handle. This usually makes the backhand grip more comfortable for players.

Take some time and learn how to *feel* the proper backhand grip. I cannot emphasize enough how important the correct grip is for learning and perfecting a solid topspin backhand drive.

In the following example, we will again break down the basic stroke into its fundamental steps, ending with a complete follow-through.

STROKE DEVELOPMENT

Follow-through Drill

Get to the contact point position. You already have the correct grip. Take small adjusting steps to position yourself with your weight on your front foot.

Without a ball, practice extending your arm to a complete follow-through and freeze. Check to be sure that your grip is still correct, that your arm is quite straight, about shoulder level, and approximately opposite your right ear, and that your racket head points toward the sky.

Backhand: To groove the stroke, freeze on the follow-through and check to make sure your position is correct.

Also make sure that your hips have made a quarter turn toward the net and that your front foot is planted firmly, with only the toes of your back foot on the ground.

This is the correct follow-through position for the backhand.

Contact–Follow-through Drill

Now add a ball to practice your hit and follow-through sequence.

Start exactly as you did in the first drill, but place your left hand over your right hand and toss a ball a few feet in front of you.

Take small adjusting steps to get into position. Stop with your weight forward. Hit the ball using the complete low to high stroke. Again freeze on your follow-through. Check your position.

Repeat several times, but be sure not to take a backswing.

Backswing–Contact–Follow-through Drill

For this step in the sequence of backhand drills, start by taking your racket back and placing your racket-hand thumb on your thigh.

Toss the ball in front of your body and take some adjusting steps.

Stop with your weight on your front foot and swing, completing your backhand stroke in a completely balanced position.

This simple drill sequence for development of the backhand will help you develop a flowing, easy shoulder rotation and will constantly reinforce muscle training for a complete follow-through. You can do this sequence of drills by yourself or with a friend tossing the ball for you.

STROKE VARIATIONS

Two-Handed Backhand

The great popularity of the two-handed backhand today is everywhere evident, from the televised broadcasts of the world class tournament professionals to the city parks where youngsters are chasing tennis balls.

Why this popularity for a stroke once believed not quite up to par? Well, for starters, there are Bjorn Borg, Chris Evert Lloyd, Jimmy Connors, Tracy Austin. . .

So obviously, if you want to become the world's best tennis player, you should use a two-handed backhander! That's obvious. Or is it?

Before you run out to start practicing this stroke, let's see what these world champions have in common.

First, they are all very quick. They have great reflexes and respond instantly.

Second, they spend hours and hours perfecting their strokes.

Third, they are predominately singles players.

Now, who should not learn to use the two-handed backhand? First, anyone who is not very quick.

Second, anyone who expects to play a lot of doubles.

Third, if you have a weak arm, you should not use a two-handed backhand because by doing so you will never strengthen your arm.

My experience has been that exactly those people who fall into the latter categories are usually the ones who want to learn to use the two-handed backhand. Initial success with this stroke is flattering, so the temptation is strong to continue using it.

But try not to succumb. The disadvantages of using a two-handed instead of a one-handed backhand outweigh the advantages.

First of all, the two-handed backhand limits your reach on wide balls. You just cannot reach as far with a two-handed stroke as you can with the traditional one-handed stroke.

A similar problem with court coverage occurs with a short ball. When the ball is short in front of a two-handed player, the player has great difficulty in handling the shot. The two-hander has a problem when he has to run forward and reach toward the ball. Even the best cannot cope with this situation. It is this very weakness in Jimmy Connors' game that many players are now successfully exploiting.

Your net play is also at a disadvantage. If you are playing the net with a two-handed backhand and the ball comes straight at your body, there is an area where you cannot cover against your body. Watch how experts like Conners jump out of the way when the ball crowds the backhand side. These highly skilled players are extremely agile and usually can make up for this deficiency of the backhand stroke.

Other problems with the two-handed backhand include the difficulty of playing a high bouncing ball, the difficulty of producing a backhand slice, and the difficulty of executing a heavy topspin return—unless you are extremely talented.

That is the bad news about the two-handed backhand. Now to the good news. When you learn the two-handed backhand, you have a devastating weapon. First, the two-handed backhand provides disguise. You really can hide the direction of your stroke because the stroke is so compact. You can wait until the last minute and then unleash the stroke, sending the ball to either side of the court and your opponent just does not have a clue as to where the ball will go.

The second advantage is that you can hit the living daylights out of the ball. The two-handed stroke generates much power.

To play the two-handed backhand, there are two approaches. You can hit the ball as a left-handed forehand drive, using the right hand for support. This is the way that Jimmy Connors plays the stroke.

The other way you may play this stroke is to hit the stroke with a regular backhand grip, with the left hand coming along for the ride, as Bjorn Borg does it. This would be my recommendation for you.

To learn the two-handed backhand I would suggest that you follow most of the rules for the forehand side. You will have a full hip and shoulder rotation unlike the normal backhand, which has little hip movement. You will face the net

Cannot easily cover wide balls

Cannot handle balls hit low in front of their feet

Once you let the second hand go, you will have no trouble with close-in shots.

at the end of the hit. Because of the restriction of the two-handed stroke, people often have to throw their bodies forward. In this stroke, this is a natural movement and it is less critical to maintain your balance throughout the hit than for the forehand.

I do have one suggestion for the two-handed players who use the Jimmy Connors' approach of hitting mainly with the left hand. Hang onto your racket all the way through the stroke with two hands. Don't let go halfway. Your stroke will be more firm and more reliable.

Backhand Slice

An important stroke to add to your repertoire is the backhand slice. It will make you a more complete tennis player. There are similarities between the movement of the racket on the back-

59

hand slice and that of the racket on the forehand slice. As you turn your shoulders and take your racket back, don't lower your racket. Open the racket face slightly and hit through the ball. This will give you a stroke that plays the ball with underspin. It will have the advantages of hanging in the air a bit longer, giving you more control of the ball and more time to recover when you are playing defensively. The backhand slice is particularly effective on a ball that bounces high. You will find it easy to control and a very worthwhile addition to your game.

One word of warning. There is a great temptation to open your hips when you slice. Stay sideways. The more sideways, the more the path of your racket will align with your intended direction for the ball.

PROBLEMS AND CORRECTIVE TECHNIQUES

Besides grip problems, snags can occur with your execution of the backhand. Here are my suggestions for coping with them.

Remember, when the mistake is similar to one which is likely to occur on the forehand side, the corrective technique is usually the same.

For example, mis-hitting on the backhand side can be corrected the same way as on the forehand. Play catch with your racket and trap the ball to establish the correct contact point for your backhand.

Leading with your elbow during the swing, slapping at the ball, losing your balance on the follow-through, or putting too much wrist into your stroke—all can be corrected with the same suggestions as those made for the forehand.

When you discover that your backswing is too large or your follow-through uncontrolled head to the fence at the side of the court and practice touching the fence behind you on the backswing and use the fence in front of you on your finish.

Perhaps you find that your racket head is opening or closing during the stroke, try balancing a coin on the racket edge.

Tennis is a balanced game to an extent, so

Backhand: Slice

Backhand: Trap the ball at contact to correct mis-hits.

Backhand: Error in hitting the ball too late and with too much wrist.

do use two hands to take your racket back for the backhand. Then let go once your forward swing starts. If you suddenly find your racket wobbling on the backswing, you most likely are neglecting to use that second hand for support. Just emphasize taking the racket back with the free hand alone for a few times so that the motion becomes grooved. You will soon find yourself using both hands naturally and releasing the support hand at the proper time.

One huge problem with the backhand is what I call the upside-down backhand. This occurs when you flip your racket over from your forehand to your backhand side using the same side of the racket to hit the ball.

Now that is a great stroke when the ball bounces high, but it restricts your stroke development, particularly when you have to play a low shot.

If you are indeed a victim of this style of backhand, put some tape on the top of your racket

Backhand: Error in hitting the ball too close to your body

Backhand: Error in opening your hips too much on the backhand.

Backhand: Upside down backhand—Don't!

shaft. Always keep that tape pointing up. Then whenever you regress and do the upside-down flip, you will quickly recognize the mistake because the tape will now be on the bottom.

To cure an unintentional slice on the backhand side, concentrate on changing the beginning of your backswing. Start your stroke much lower. You may actually want to place your thumb on your thigh and then swing from low to high. If you are inclined to be poetic, the following will help you remember this:

Thumb on the thigh,
Finish toward the ssthkky!

SUMMARY

The backhand is at first difficult to learn. The grip is unfamiliar. You don't have enough strength in your extensor muscles. The strangeness of swinging from your left side makes you hesitant about playing the stroke. Once you get the feeling of a backhand, once you start developing a little confidence, you will be pleasantly surprised about how quickly the stroke will grow. My own experience is that most people eventually find their backhand to be their preferable side. They actually have more confidence in their backhand than in their forehand.

So practice the backhand. Particularly in practice situations or in match play when you are stronger than your opponent, favor your backhand. Don't run around your backhand; if you do, you will be unable to play the stroke under stress situations. So start off right away and use your backhand as often as you can so that your confidence will grow.

HIGH BACKHANDS

There are three ways to play a high backhand.

One, come up on the ball. Two, slice the ball. Three, flick your wrist and hit down on the ball.

Number three is no good. Use it only rarely.

Number two you use to keep the ball deep, or hit short angles.

Number one you use when you want to give your opponent some of his own medicine.

To play a slice off a high bouncing ball, take the racket back high next to your left ear. Open the racket face and hit through the ball with a slightly downward follow-through.

When your opponent stays back, take your racket back high. Keep the racket face on edge and finish even higher than at the point of contact.

This will give the ball some topspin, and if you can hit it to the baseline, your opponent will have a tough high bouncing ball with which to contend. It is quite a difficult shot to master, but well worth learning.

Backhand: Hit a high-bouncing backhand by keeping your racket face on edge and finishing even higher than your point of contact.

Volley

4.

You can play tennis without being able to volley. You may stand on the baseline and just poop the ball back all day. But it will be very boring. For you, your opponent, and any spectators.

The volley is the shot you need to finesse the point. The serve puts the ball in play. Groundstrokes give you a chance to rally the ball. And then, when in position, you can attack the net. This is where a good, reliable volley is essential.

Funny thing is, the volley is incredibly easy to learn. It is a very simple stroke because the backswing is reduced to almost zero. And, there is very little follow-through to the stroke.

YOUR POSITION ON COURT

Where should you stand? When you are playing doubles and your partner is serving, you should be about a yard or so off the singles sideline and perhaps a yard or two back from the net. But, this position will depend upon the strength of your partner's serve. If your partner has a very poor serve, you ought to crowd the alley more. If your partner serves wide to the opponent's forehand side, again you should crowd the alley. If your partner serves to the backhand side, you can move a little bit more into the center of the court. If your partner serves a high bouncing ball to the opponent's backhand, you can even venture farther into the center of the court. So, the kind of serve that your partner is capable of determines where you will stand.

A second factor in determining where you will stand is your opponent's ability to return serve. If you have an opponent who returns serve very well, again you will take a position closer to the net and closer to the sidelines. As you discover that your opponent doesn't have the ability to make an aggressive return, you can be more

venturesome at net and take more chances.

When your partner is receiving serve, then your waiting position will be about a yard from the center service line and the service line. That position gives you a good position to defend against the opposing net player.

YOUR BODY POSITION

Perhaps the most important clue that I can give you on how to stand is to *crouch*. Don't stand up straight. Crouch low enough by bending your knees so that you cannot see the service line on the other side. Then you will have a good ready position. Now you can go from left to right and pounce on any ball.

Volley: Good position at the net.

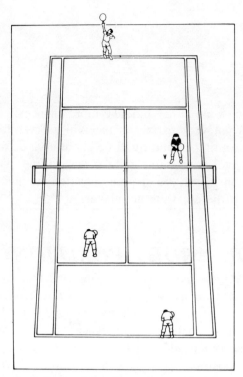

A. Volley position: If your partner has a weak serve, you should crowd the alley.

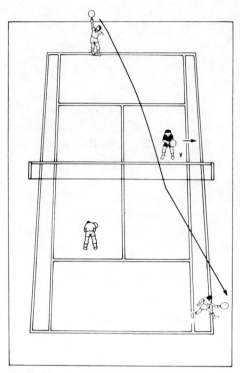

C. Volley position: If your partner serves wide to your opponent's forehand court, you can crowd the alley safely.

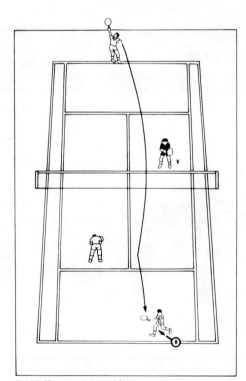

B. Volley position: If your partner serves to your opponent's backhand side, you can move toward the center of the court.

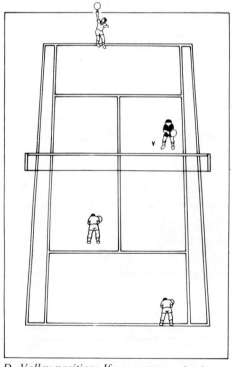

D. Volley position: If your opponent returns serve well, your position should be relatively closer to the net and closer to the sidelines.

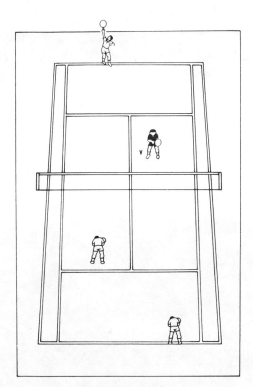

E. Volley position: Likewise, if your opponent does not return serve well, you should be able to be more aggressive, cover more court space toward the center of the court, and farther back from the net.

Volley: Hold the racket like a steering wheel and block the ball to see how firm and stable the stroke should be

Volley: Use your regular forehand and backhand grips for firmness when you initially start to learn the volley.

THE GRIP (also see Chapter 19)

Although I recommend that you use the Continental grip—a grip halfway between an Eastern forehand grip and a backhand grip—for the volley, it is not a bad idea at first to use your regular forehand grip to give stability to your forehand volley.

To understand just how stable you should be when you volley on the forehand side, try the following. Hold on to the racket face with two hands on the rim and keep the racket in front of your face. Just block the ball as it comes to you.

Volley: To learn the forehand volley, first hold your left hand in front of the racket and catch the ball
Then hold the left hand in back of the racket and try to catch the ball through the strings.

CHANGING GRIPS FOR THE VOLLEY

Beginners need to change grips from forehand to backhand and meet the ball with the full racket face.

As players become more advanced, they can open the racket face more and hit a glancing underspin stroke.

To play such a glancing stroke it is not necessary to make as great a grip change as in the beginning. At this stage the player's wrist and forearm are also more educated and the grip change is very slight; in many instances there is no discernible change in the hand position.

The most common complaint is, "I don't have time to change my grip." Of course you have time.

While you are moving the racket into position make the grip change. Thus it is less a problem of not having time than one of not remembering.

Your volley skills will improve dramatically with systematic predictable practice. At first practice only alternate forehands and backhands until the grip change becomes almost automatic. Only then do reflex drills.

By that time you may not need a big grip change anymore because your stroke pattern will have become sound.

HOW TO HIT A FOREHAND VOLLEY

Now hold the racket's handle with your regular forehand grip. Hold your left hand in front of the racket at the contact point and catch the ball as it comes to you. Practice by having someone throw you a ball a few times. Now, hold your left hand *behind* the racket face (this will also stop you from swinging back) and try to catch the ball again. Of course it is impossible

because the strings meet the ball first.

Now add footwork to your volley. As the ball comes toward you, take a step in with your left foot. This exercise will give you a very good idea of how to play a forehand volley.

Two good clues for hitting a solid volley are knowing that the butt of your racket will be pointing toward your left toe while you are hitting the ball properly on the forehand side, and, conversely, knowing that the butt of your racket will be pointing toward your right toe when you hit the backhand volley properly. These two checks will always tell you that the angle of your racket for a chest-high volley is correct.

As you become a more experienced volleyer, you will not change your grip from forehand to backhand any more. You will most likely use an in-between grip, the Continental grip for your

Volley: To learn the backhand volley, first block the ball with the racket as though it were a steering wheel to establish a firm hit.

volleys. Using just one grip for both volleys, you will put a bit more underspin on the ball; and this grip will give more control and depth to your shots.

HOW TO HIT A BACKHAND VOLLEY

For the backhand volley, you need a firm grip. At first, as you are learning the volley, make substantial grip changes from the forehand and backhand sides. How do you do it? Just turn your hand from your forehand grip until the knuckle of the first finger is on top of the racket. You will get much support from your thenar, the fleshy part of your palm just below the thumb.

Again, I must emphasize the same points for the backhand volley as the forehand. Hold your racket as though it were the steering wheel of an automobile. Punch one or two balls holding the

Volley: Footwork on the volley depends on where the ball is hit, For a wide shot, step and cross over to hit the ball. For a short shot in front of you, step in. On occasions, it is permissible to volley off the right foot.

racket this way. Gradually slide your hand down the racket until it is at the end of the handle. Now give the ball a punch while holding the fist of your left hand against the back of the racket face. Your left hand will inhibit the backswing so you won't swing back too far. As a second step, use ing for this "block." Put your racket down for a minute and just pretend that you are a policeman, holding up your hand to block traffic. In this position, have a partner toss you a ball. You block it with your hand. That is your volley motion. Now hold the racket face with your hand

Volley: Forehand Learning Sequence.
Block traffic like a policeman. Then block traffic with your hand behind the racket strings.
Move your hand down the shaft halfway and block the traffic again.
Finally, move your hand all the way down the shaft and volley the ball.

your left hand to support the throat of the racket and solidly jab the ball. Try not to move your wrist in any way. Last, step into the ball as you hit the volley.

When you are hitting your volleys, remember that the stroke is short and staccato. Just take a short punch at the ball.

BLOCK THE BALL TO VOLLEY

For some players, my second approach to learning to volley increases awareness and feel-

across the strings and block the ball again. Move your hand halfway down the shaft and block another tossed ball. Remember to use the same blocking motion. Don't start to add a backswing Finally, hold your racket normally and repeat the same forehand volley motion.

The backhand routine works much the same way. First block a tossed ball with your thumb. Go ahead. Just hold your thumb out to meet the ball. Then hold the racket face with your thumb behind the strings and block another ball. Have your hand halfway down the racket shaft and repeat the backhand volley. Finally, move your

Volley: Backhand Volley Learning Sequence.
First block the ball with your thumb.
Then block the ball with your thumb behind the racket strings.
Move your hand down the shaft halfway, adjust your grip and block the ball.
Move your hand all the way down the shaft and hit a firm backhand volley!

LOW VOLLEYS

Bend Your Knees, Twenty Dollars, Please is the title of a popular book on tennis.

When it refers to low volleys the title is apt. Whenever the knees are stiff and the racket droops, invariably the ball will go into the net or over the baseline, or pop up for an easy put-away by the opponent.

Stiff knees usually bring about a droopy racket head. In addition, the tendency to swing at the ball and to close the racket face is a contributory problem.

Low volleys can be vastly improved by practice. Most players practice their volleys at net but neglect to include those volleys that are played from close to the service line.

Clues to remember: Keep the knees flexible. Open the racket face and use a short backswing.

hand to the normal backhand grip and volley with confidence.

VOLLEY FOOTWORK

To improve your volleying, practice these footwork patterns. Have a practice partner feed you the ball, close to your body so you don't have to move. Then, one step with your right foot; then further, so that you have to reach with your left foot; then still further, so that you have to take two steps with your right foot; then left foot. Step away with your left foot when the ball comes right at you. And finally, the easy one where you step in and finish the point.

If you practice these variables of footwork, you will become a more consistent and confident volleyer.

Using the footwork pattern that I suggest here, you should be able to cover almost every possibility except the emergency shot where you will just have to dive for the ball.

PROBLEMS AND CORRECTIVE TECHNIQUES

The most common and devastating mistake in the volley is overswinging at the ball—no matter how often I tell players:

"Keep the racket out in front!"

"Block the ball!"

"Punch the ball, don't swing back!"

Players take the racket back too far. The farther back you take your racket, the more you will often hear that dull klunk as you hit the ball near the edge of the frame. Imagine your embarrassment of going into your pro shop and having to tell the pro, "Say, my strings are brand new, but the frame is worn out."

Here is a corrective suggestion that will cure overswinging very quickly. Stand against the backfence or a wall or any solid object. Have a friend toss you a ball. If you try to take a backswing, you will hit your racket against the fence, a jolting reminder to reduce your backswing on the volley.

Another way to stop overswinging on the volley is to practice with a headband around your forearms. Headbands are not as common as they used to be. A few years ago everyone used headbands, but some spare headbands should still be lying around. Just put a headband over your forearms and start volleying. You will be surprised at how a headband restricts your backswing.

If these two approaches do not help, I have one last suggestion. I remember teaching a young tennis player, Marcy Louie, who eventually became a ranking player in the United States. She is still playing on the Avon circuit. She hated to

Volley: When the ball comes straight at you, quickly move your left foot out of the way so that you can meet the ball squarely.

Volley: Use a backfence to block your backswing
if you discover you are taking your racket back too far on the volley.

volley and always had a big backswing. The way we cured Marcy's backswing was to tie a rope from her racket to the net. Then she could not swing back. A couple of times since then I have used the same method and it has been helpful.

Another common mistake is dropping the racket head as you volley. The ball comes low. You instinctively drop the racket head. You then have to scoop the ball. The ball surely will pop up and out on the other side. If it doesn't pop up and out, it will surely pop right up into the racket of your opponent, who will put it away for a winner. When the ball is low, bend your knees. Practice bending your knees. Don't be shy. Bend your knees to such an extent that you actually sit down and touch the ground with your right knee

on the forehand and left knee on the backhand. Once you have practiced sitting down all the way on your knee, you will be surprised at how solid your volley feels on low shots.

Another volley mistake that marks a mediocre player is using a "windshield-wiper" volley. That is the volley where you play a normal forehand volley, then when you hit a backhand volley you turn your hand upside down. For both strokes you use the same face of the racket. Once you have learned to windshield-wipe the volley, you will be hard put to cure it because the action feels so good and you like those solid hits on the backhand side when the ball is about three or four feet above the net. But when the ball is net-high or so, you just cannot play the ball. And if the ball is lower than the net, it is guaranteed that the windshield-wiper volley will send the ball into the net. So if you are a windshield-wiper and you play the ball using the same racket face to hit both forehand and backhand volleys, you should change it.

A good way to correct this kind of volley is to stick a piece of tape on the edge of the racket so that whenever you hit the ball properly, you will see the tape on the top of your racket. Whether a forehand hit or a backhand hit, the tape should always be visible on top. If you turn the racket upside down, the red tape will be underneath and you will know immediately that you used the windshield-wiper stroke again.

Another suggestion is a practice technique that should help you promote a solid volley. Many players hit a volley and then let their racket go upward after they meet the ball. This makes for a very weak shot. The way to cure this problem is to touch the net with your racket imme-diately after you hit your volley. As a practice suggestion, this routine is valuable for people who just pop the ball up.

SUMMARY

The volley is an essential for singles after you open up the court, so that you can go into the net and finesse the point. It is possible to play singles without volleying, but it makes for a very boring game. In doubles, if you don't have a volley, you are not playing doubles. You are playing some kind of hybrid singles.

So learn to volley. Get into the net. Don't be scared. If you keep your racket up and out in front of your body, you will be able to prepare very quickly. Often players are afraid that they may get hit. I have rarely seen players hit when they have the racket in front of their face. Don't

Volley: Don't drop the racket head to scoop a low ball on the volley. (Bend your knees and get down for it instead.)

Volley: Bend your knees,—touch the ground if necessary, to get a very low volley.

Volley: Don't use a windshield wiper volley!

swing back. Keep the racket out in front and you will lose all fear of the volley. Set your racket head early. If you get set up early, you will find that the volley is no problem.

Again, don't look for power in the stroke. Just think of your racket as a really firm wall, to block the ball and angle it away from the opponent, and you will very likely win more points than your opponent with the big flashy windup.

THE LOB VOLLEY

Occasionally in good doubles, someone will successfully hit a lob volley. The ball will loft over both opponents' rackets at the net and bounce deep into their backcourt. This shot is usually an outright winner.

To hit a lob volley, you must tilt your racket face open to the sky just as you are about to hit your punch volley.

The danger of this stroke is that if you do not get enough height on the ball, you are a sitting duck for an overhead hit at you from close range.

THE SPECIALTY SHOTS

PART II

5.

Lob

"Yours, partner!"

" 'Yours,' you've got to be kidding! Get it yourself!"

Whenever people are playing tennis on a social level, and someone lobs, ninety percent of the time the lobber will win the point—and occasion an argument between the opposing teammates.

I have never understood why people do not improve their overheads in response to this statistic, or why people don't routinely lob more often. They just don't. As a result, for most social tennis players, even those on the intermediate-advanced level, the lob is a devastating weapon. So use it. You will win many points with an accurate lob. People just don't have overheads that are as good as they think they are.

Once you have learned the serve, the return of serve, and the volley, you must learn the specialty shots of tennis. Your dimensions as a tennis player will grow if you can play approach shots, half volleys, drop shots, and overhead smashes. You will sharpen your skill and enjoy the game more fully.

You'll find yourself a step above the player who has no midcourt game. And if you can lob, the world will be yours.

WHEN TO USE

The lob is an extremely versatile shot. A wonderful defensive reserve to have on call when you are pressed and out of position on the court, the lob also can be an effective offensive shot on occasion.

Defensively, the lob can get you out of hot water. If you are drawn wide off the court retrieving a shot or if you find yourself being run from side to side by your opponent, try a lob.

The lob will give you a breather and a chance to recover your court position. The lob will save the point for one more stroke, and give your opponent the opportunity of making an error.

Lob *deep* to your opponent's backcourt, particularly to the backhand side, to lower your chances of having to deal with an overhead smash return. In the event that your opponent does hit an overhead back, at least you will have recovered to the center of the court. Lob also when you have been forced back far off the court chasing a high bouncing lob. A drive would probably be cut off by an opponent advancing to the net.

As an attack weapon, lob when your opponent is crowding the net and then approach the net yourself. Your opponent now is likely to hit you an easy shot, either a lob return or a weak drive.

The topspin lob is a devastatingly effective offensive weapon. Correctly hit, the topspin lob will skim over the opposing player's racket head, just out of reach. Upon landing, the heavy spin will cause the ball to shoot toward the back fence. Not even the best of players can chase it down for a return.

TV announcers always complain about the topspin lob. "Well, he just made one of those low-percentage topspin lobs. Don't you people in TV land try it. It is too difficult for you."

Nonsense. Add it to your repertoire of strokes. Even when you hit it badly, the spin will make it a tough shot for the opponent to handle.

The regular lob is similar to other ground strokes in method, except that the face of the racket is open during the stroke. Open racket face means that the face of the racket is tilted toward the sky. Your grip does not change. Use your regular forehand or backhand grip when hitting a lob. All you have to do is turn your wrist to open your racket face.

Lob: Illustration of an on edge and open racket faces
On edge   *Open*

STROKE PRODUCTION

The Grip

Use your regular forehand or backhand grip.

The Stance

Assume the regular groundstroke waiting position.

The Turn

The first thing you do when preparing to hit a lob is turn your shoulders. Pivot and shift your weight to the side to which the ball is coming.

Racket Preparation

For the forehand and backhand lob, take your racket back and down. Do not change your grip from your usual groundstroke grip. Turn your wrist to open the racket face slightly. Once you establish the degree of your wrist turn, keep the wrist position the same throughout the rest of the stroke.

Adjusting Steps

Move your feet quickly with short steps to reach a hitting position.

The Hit

Ideally hit the ball slightly in front of your body, about thigh-high.

The Follow-through

Complete your follow-through carefully. Don't cut it short. The longer the racket face goes in the direction of the ball, the more you will feel that you can control its direction, height, and speed.

Lob: Hold the racket face open when you take the racket back and when you swing through to hit the ball.

Forehand lob: Hit the ball and follow through with an open racket face. Note the open racket face.

Backhand lob: On the backhand side the racket face also is open on the contact and follow-through.

Lob: Topspin lob sequence for forehand

THE TOPSPIN LOB

The topspin lob is a devastating weapon—a good addition to your tennis repertoire. Though a supposedly difficult shot to learn, the topspin lob is surprisingly simple when approached by means of understandable steps.

The topspin lob differs from the regular lob in its *exaggerated follow-through*. On the forehand side, your topspin lob will *finish with the racket head behind your head on your racket-arm side*. Your elbow will be bent. On the backhand side, your *topspin lob will also finish with the racket head behind your head on your racket-arm side*.

Stroke Production

Grip—regular forehand or backhand grip.

Stance—regular waiting position.

Turn—turn your shoulders and pivot.

Racket preparation—same as for groundstrokes, except open the face of the racket by turning your hand slightly, but do not alter your grip.

Adjusting steps—Take small quick steps to position.

Hit—*brush up sharply on the ball to impart topspin.*

Follow-through—Finish with the racket behind your head on your racket side.

Lob: Topspin lob sequence for the backhand.

Lob: Topspin lob learning sequence for the forehand.

Hold the ball between the net and the racket

Pull the racket up sharply

Finish with the racket cocked behind your head and on your racket side

Learning Sequence

Four easily mastered steps will help you learn how to hit the topspin lob.

First, hold a ball between the net and your tennis racket. Pull your racket up sharply and finish with your racket cocked behind your head on your racket side.

Next, stand a few feet from the net. Hold your racket on edge. Drop a ball and after it bounces, brush up sharply as before and finish again with the racket cocked behind your head.

Third, open your racket face and again brush up sharply on the ball. Again finish behind your back.

Finally, have a partner feed you the ball. Execute the stroke as you have practiced and you will send the ball smartly over your partner's head and out of reach.

SUMMARY

The maligned lob is really an important weapon. When anyone says, "I don't like to play him. He lobs. . .," what that player is really saying is, "I don't like to play him. He is testing my nervous overhead smash."

An accurate lob, played judiciously, is a great addition to your game. People who lob get much more enjoyment from the game because they are setting up more tactical situations. When someone approaches the net and you lob the ball, you are using an alternative response. Rather than trying to pass your opponent, choose occasionally to go over your opponent's head. This will make your game much more versatile tactically.

Lob: Learning Sequence for the Backhand Topspin Lob.

Hold the ball between the net and the racket

Pull the racket up sharply

Finish with the racket cocked behind your head and on your racket side

6.

Overhead Smash

The overhead smash is everyone's favorite. Trouble is, everyone tries to hit the living daylights out of the ball and that results in a low success ratio.

Placement of the overhead smash is more important than power. Usually, when you are readying to hit an overhead, the court is yours, so don't overhit. Meet the ball high in the air. When the ball goes into the net instead of into the court, you have let the ball fall too low before hitting.

So reach up to hit the ball at the highest possible point. Hit the ball right over your head for the correct contact point on the smash. If you let the ball get behind you, you are likely to hit the ball long. Should you hit the ball too far in front, the ball will go into the net.

STROKE PRODUCTION

The Grip

The grip is the same as your service grip.

Overhead: Illustration of a high backhand smash, angled for a winner.

Overhead: Waiting position

The Turn

The first movement you make when you realize that you are getting a lob is to *turn your body sideways to the net*. While stepping back with your right foot, lift your free hand into the air and point at the ball for balance. Abbreviate your backswing and drop the racket behind your back and hold it on edge. *Don't take a full circular backswing* as you do in the serve. The timing is too difficult.

The Waiting Position

Your waiting position for the overhead is the same as that for the volley. Face the net with your knees slightly bent. Be low and ready to move, your weight evenly distributed and well forward. Hold your racket in front of you at an upward angle.

Overhead: Turn immediately.

The Follow-through

Complete your overhead by letting your racket follow through to your opposite side. At the completion of the stroke your shoulders will have rotated forward. Your weight will be well forward. Your eyes will be following the direction of your shot.

Recovery

Immediately return to the net waiting position.

Overhead: Hit at your most fully extended point.

Overhead: Complete your overhead by bringing your racket all the way through to your opposite side.

Footwork

Adjust your position by taking small quick steps. Stop when you are directly *under the ball*.

The Hit

Reach high, as in the serve. Your weight transfers to your front foot at this point. You are fully extended at contact.

Overhead: Learning Sequence

Step one: Start with your racket behind your back, sight and catch the ball with your free hand.

OVERHEAD SMASH STROKE DEVELOPMENT EXERCISES

To acquire the skill of consistently hitting a good overhead smash, you must grasp the basic steps of the stroke. Reduce the overhead to its simplest movements and then rebuild your stroke bit by bit.

Through the years I have obtained good results by building the overhead around a correct contact point. Then I add the follow-through to the stroke production and from this point work backward to the preparation.

Step two: Start with your racket behind your back, sight the ball with your free hand, reach up and contact the ball and stop. Don't follow through.

Step three: Start with your racket behind your back, sight the ball, reach up and hit the ball and slowly follow through.

Step 3. Repeat as above. This time stop when you contact the ball, slowly follow through.

Step 4. Repeat the above step, but do not stop at contact. Instead, move under the ball, reach up and contact the ball, and without stopping, *slowly follow through.*

Overhead Fast Turn Exercise

Stand in the waiting position at the net. Say to yourself, "Turn." Then turn your shoulders and immediately step back and transfer your weight to your back foot. Take your racket back behind your head. Take two or three adjusting steps. Go through a shadow motion of hitting the ball.

Overhead Preparation and Complete Stroke Exercise

Start in the waiting volley position. Turn your body into position for hitting. Have your partner lob the ball. Hit carefully and slowly at first. Follow through. Add speed once consistency develops.

SUMMARY

During the overhead exercises for stroke production, be conscious of carefully grooving both your stroke and gauging the ball's descent. Synchronize the hitting with the ball's descent.

PROBLEM AND CORRECTION

Your biggest problem with your overhead will be hitting the ball too late. To overcome this tendency, try pointing at the ball until the moment you start to swing. This should help you get in position under the ball and reach up early enough to hit the ball before it drops too low.

Overhead Contact Point Exercise

Step 1. Stand sideways to the net with your racket on edge behind your back. Your weight is on your back foot. Extend your free arm upward to sight the ball. *Move under* and catch a lobbed ball a few times.

Step 2. Repeat the above, starting in the same ready-to-hit position. This time when the ball is lobbed, move under the ball, reach up, and just contact the ball. Do not follow through.

Step four: Repeat the sequence all in one motion.

7.

Drop Shot

Every kind of shot will give you a different kind of pleasure. A clean passing shot, a service ace, and a jumping overhead smash will make you feel like macho man. But a drop shot, a delicate little ball that just clears the net and comes to a dead stop, is the essence of touch.

Everybody should have a drop shot. When you have mastered a drop shot, you have transcended the slugger's world. You have transcended the pusher's world. You have added the dimension of touch to your game. Everybody who can play a drop shot at the right moment knows the satisfaction it gives.

The addition of a drop shot to Chris Evert Lloyd's game was most important to her success in top-level tennis. Before she had a drop shot, she would run her opponents' from side to side. Then when they hit short, Chris would pummel the ball for a winner into either corner.

But her opponents grew wise. They would wait until the very moment that she started her forward swing and then would dash to one side or the other. This gave them a fifty-fifty chance of guessing right.

Then Chris added the drop shot and reduced her opponents' chances to one in three of guessing right.

The nicest thing about the drop shot is that it is very easy to learn. Once you have learned how to volley the ball, you can also play the drop shot. In other words, the drop shot and the volley share the same characteristics.

The drop shot is virtually a volley that is *played just after the ball has bounced.* If you follow the suggestions of how the stroke should develop, you can easily add the drop shot to your game.

STROKE PRODUCTION

To hit a drop shot, imagine you are hitting your groundstroke as a volley and you will find that the drop shot is simple to learn.

Hit a few volleys a little further back from the net—about the service line. Practice your forehand and your backhand volleys. Concentrate on meeting the ball out in front and playing it with a slight downward jab.

Now repeat the action after the ball has bounced. When you see the ball coming, step quickly to the ball and jab at it. Don't let your racket go back. Keep your follow-through short.

The Grip

Use your regular groundstroke grips for the forehand and the backhand drop shots.

Court Position

Usually you will hit a drop shot when you are inside the baseline and your opponent is in the far backcourt.

Contact

To hit the drop shot, give the ball a short and slightly downward jab.

WHEN TO USE DROP SHOTS

The drop shot is primarily used in singles. There are specific dos and don'ts about its use. First of all, rarely attempt a drop shot when you are behind your baseline. Conversely, the shot is most effective when you are inside the baseline and your opponent is far back and out of position in his court.

The drop shot is of course particularly effective against slow opponents and opponents who are out of condition.

Drop shot: Hit the ball with a jab!

Use the drop shot judiciously!!! Misuse can be fatal. . .to you. A drop shot that lands on the service line or beyond is not a drop shot. The criterion for a good drop shot is one that bounces at least twice or, even better, three times before crossing the service line.

Perhaps the most important feature of a drop shot is disguise. If you telegraph your intent to drop-shot, the point is as good as lost. You must be able to hide the stroke. So if you make a quick and early shoulder turn that resembles the turn you make when about to play a drive or a slice, you have disguise working for you. If you can disguise the stroke, you can make a winner out of it. But if you can't, your opponent will read your intentions, run in, and easily knock it off.

8.

Approach Shot

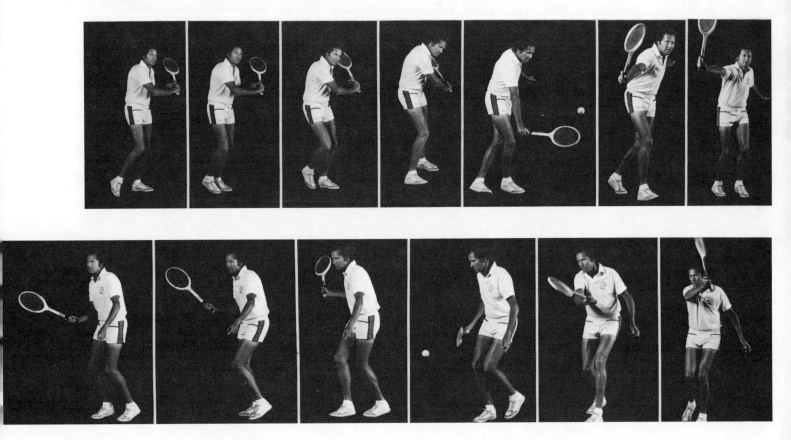

Once you have a backcourt game of solid groundstrokes and have also learned how to hit volleys and overheads, the next addition to your tennis game should be a reliable approach shot so that you can move from the baseline to the net, where the action is.

The important feature of the approach shot is that, unlike most tennis shots, ball contact occurs while your are moving. Unlike a regular groundstroke, the approach shot does not require that you have your weight set before hitting the ball.

Although you hit the approach shot on the run, body balance still is important. When you hit an approach shot, keep your upper body quiet and concentrate on carrying through a smooth stroke on the forehand or the backhand side. To achieve this smooth balance while in motion, *controlled footwork* is necessary.

Most approach shots are sliced and directed down the line so as to give one ample opportunity to prepare for the volley. A cross-court shot will open up the court and give an opponent too much of an opportunity to pass you. A topspin shot is not bad as an approach shot, but there is a strong tendency to hit the ball short.

STROKE PRODUCTION

As you run toward the net, take your racket back for a slice. Run in and meet the ball a little ahead of your right foot. Stay in motion.

This requires judgment, anticipation, and practice, but you don't have to think about everything. The computer in your brain will make the necessary adjustments for you as you repeat and repeat the movement.

Approach shot: Split step sequence on the forehand approach shot

Approach shot: Approach shot footwork on the backhand side

Slice the ball down the line (or cross-court once in a while).

Keep running forward. Now stop with a split step to your volley position just as your opponent prepares to hit his return. At first you will stop too late and get passed. Or you will stop too early and not have good court position. Keep practicing to get the timing right.

Backhand Approach Shot

The backhand approach shot offers you the challenge of some fancy footwork, what I call a "carioca" step.

As you run to the net for your backhand approach shot, take your racket back to slice the ball. Run with your shoulders somewhat sideways to the net. Just at the moment you hit the ball, cross your back leg behind your front. This footwork will help you keep your body sideways to the net throughout the follow-through. Hit through the ball. Direct the ball down the line.

Keep running until your opponent is prepared to return the shot, then stop with a split step to be ready for your volley. Time your split stepping to coincide with your opponent's stroke preparation. Now you are ready to move to hit your volley.

PRACTICE DRILL

To become proficient at playing approach shots, you need much practice at grooving the stroke. You will need a partner for this drill, preferably one who would also like to work on the approach shot.

Alternate hitting and feeding. First, your partner should start the ball from the baseline, hitting a short ball. You will then run in and play the approach shot, split step, and volley.

Then your partner will take his turn. Work on the forehand and backhand sides.

SPLIT STEP

The purpose of the split step is to put you into the volley position immediately. You use the split step to stop your forward motion. You hop, spreading your legs comfortably apart to place yourself in the familiar waiting and ready position to volley.

Half Volley

9.

The half volley says a lot about you as a tennis player. Because, the half volley is really the basis of a good forehand drive. In fact, the half volley is an abbreviated forehand and backhand drive. If you cannot make a successful half volley, your forehand drive is faulty. If you can produce a half volley soundly, your forehand drive is most likely also sound.

You will have to make half volleys on two occasions. One is when you are caught on the baseline as your opponent plays a deep shot, and you have to meet the ball on the rise and play it back steadily. The second occasion for the half volley is when you are going toward the net and

Half Volley Stroke Production Forehand
Step one: Block the ball with your racket.

Step two: Reach out on the follow-through.

113

Half Volley Stroke Production: Backhand
Step one: Meet the ball just after it touches the ground.

Step two: Then reach out on the follow-through.

your opponent catches you midcourt and you have to play the ball off your feet.

You don't have to make a winning shot. All you do when you make a half volley is play the ball down the line and get in position as quickly as you can.

If you want a good picture of a half volley, watch an experienced shortstop field a line drive. Whenever I see a shortstop, I invariably think, "Boy, that guy would make a great half-volleyer. His knees are bent. He is low. He doesn't take a backswing and he blocks the ball firmly out in front of his body." Those are the characteristics of a good half volley.

Another example of a half volley is a drop-kick. The instant the ball touches the ground, you kick. It is a little beat-one-two/one-two. Bounce and hit, with no discernible delay in between. If you can get the bounce-hit beat, then you have the half-volley rhythm.

STROKE PRODUCTION

The stroke can be learned very quickly and easily if you follow these steps.

Step 1. Have someone toss you the ball and block it with your hand.

Step 2. Hold your racket in your hand and without any backswing just block the ball as it hits the ground.

Step 3. As the ball hits the ground, meet the ball and just push your arm straight forward and try to keep the face of the racket parallel to the net as long as you can.

That is the half volley. There is nothing more to it.

PROBLEMS

One of the most common mistakes in the half volley is taking too big a backswing. When such critical timing is involved, taking too big a backswing will destroy your timing. Remember, therefore, to reduce the half-volley backswing to almost zero. The timing should be bounce-hit and you will have a good point of contact.

Another problem is not bending your knees on the half volley. When you drop your racket head, you will scoop the ball. Exaggerate and bend your knees more than necessary. It will help you to position your racket better for a solid contact point.

PART III

THE GAME

10.

Tactics

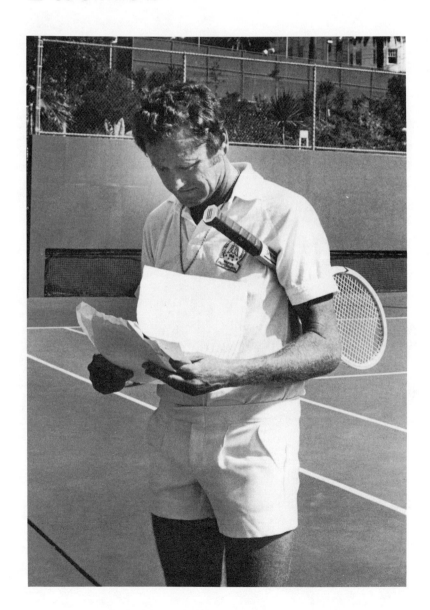

The very mention of tennis tactics usually conjures up an image of a court drawn on a blackboard and covered with a formidable array of lines and squiggles representing possible strategy-and-response situations. Unfortunately, this fanciful classroom picture has very little to do with the reality of actual on-court tactics, simply because there are so many different levels of play.

The problem is that all tennis players are not created equal and there will always remain certain areas of execution that are beyond many aspirants' abilities. For this reason, a discussion of tactics has to be tailor-made to each player's skills. Once one identifies his particular level, a certain set of tactics can be implemented to ensure the best chance of winning among your peers.

A service tactic for the relative novice obviously will not be as effective against the more advanced, but it will prove a winner against a player of comparable skill. To a novice, the only relevant service tactic is to *get the ball into the court*. Why such simple advice? Because statistics bear it out.

Statistics of thousands of matches played by players of different skill levels show that novice players miss on the average over sixty percent of their returns. It is as basic as that. Just get the ball into the court, no matter how punily. If you never double-fault, the odds are three to two that you will win the point.

This is easy enough for beginners, of course, but once you start moving up the ladder to the intermediate level, tactics with a little more finesse will have to be introduced. At this stage the ability to direct the serve to either the forehand or the backhand side will give the server a decided advantage, particularly if the serve is delivered deep and close to the corners. This will normally force the opponent to back up and make a weak return. Among intermediates, speed is of little consequence; what counts most is consistency.

It is only when we get into the more advanced level of play that speed and spin enter into service tactics. Now—and only now—one should count on being able to pull his opponent wide with a slice serve or to twist a high bounce to the backhand. And then there's the ultimate weapon: the cannon ball, a serve so devastatingly fast that your opponent has barely moved as the ball whizzes by. This is the pinnacle of tennis—being able to whack an ace when most needed.

BASIC TACTICS

Remember this basic progression of tactics: (1) as a novice, *get the ball into the court;* (2) as an intermediate, *direct the ball from side to side;* (3) as a more skillful player, *hit the ball deep into the corners;* and (4) as an advanced player, *go for spin and speed.*

Maybe all this seems very apparent, but players often forget their skill level. Nearly every novice, for instance, tries to change the sequence around. First comes the mighty windup, accompanied by the grunt and groan, and then the ball ends up against the back fence. For the second serve, some poopdy-poop is delivered. If these are your tactics, you are doomed to mediocrity. Change them.

What about tactics for returning the serve? Almost the same set of tactics described for the serve should be used when receiving serve. In the early stages, just try to get the ball back with consistency. Then vary your return from corner to corner. As you are able to add pace to your stroke, you can aim the ball deep and then come to the net to put away your opponent's weak return.

Once you can force a weak return from your opponent, take the net with an approach shot, and follow it with a winning volley, then you have truly progressed to an advanced level of play.

Playing at the net is, of course, an important ingredient of the skillful player's overall game. All you need know is a bit of elementary geometry, and one additional thing: good judgment. The first part is easy. Your basic tactic is to hit an approach shot down the line, go to the net, and finish the point with a winning cross-court volley to the open court. The only snag comes with the second part: be sure to make your cross-court volley a winner because if you don't, your opponent will run the ball down and pass you.

Here enters judgment. Unless you are sure that you will hit a winner, don't volley cross-court. Instead, hold the line, hit the ball back down the line, and go cross-court only when you are certain of a winning shot.

DOUBLE TACTICS

In discussing winning doubles strategies, it is important to know that hitters rarely win in doubles. Statistically for every winner two errors are made.

Doubles is a game of position play, ball placement and finesse of stroke. A good serve can win the point outright or maintain your positional advantage. A good placement of the return keeps the opponent from winning the point outright or taking on offensive position.

The importance of a good first serve in doubles cannot be overstressed. On the average, 18% of first serves are outright winners. Only about 1% of second serves win the point outright.

Furthermore, it is likely that the serving team will win 80% of the points when the first serve is good, but this ratio drops off to only about 48% on the second serve.

When your first serve goes in, your partner at net has a field day and can expect to poach successfully almost 70% of the time. When you miss your first serve, your partner has only about a 10% chance of making a successful poach.

But that's not all. When you miss your first serve, the receivers will get to the net six times more often than when the first serve is good. The message is clear: get your first serve in!

On the deuce side, serve the ball down the middle so that your net partner won't have to worry about guarding the alley and your opponents will have only minimal openings.

On the ad court, serve wide because your partner has a forehand volley waiting if the receiver goes down the line. Another good tactic is to serve straight at the receiver.

Of course, in doubles you must follow your serve into the net. Take something off the ball so that you can get in a bit closer and then be sure to make that first volley. The success of this first shot will determine whether your team will be on the offense or defense. Try to avoid overhitting the first volley after the serve. It is far better to make the shot and then move in for the put-away.

Be prepared to volley more than once. Don't overplay the first volley and find yourself unprepared for the second volley. When the receiver stays back, volley deep and close to the middle of the court. When the receiver is coming in, volley to his feet. Don't go for angles with your volley unless you are really forcing the point. Your opponent can easily hit a winner from an angled shot which does not challenge him.

As the server's partner, you should develop a sense of how to drift across the net and poach. You must also be alert for a high return which of course should be smacked away for a winner.

Remember, when the ball is hit down the middle and you and your partner are both at the net, the forehand player generally takes the shot. (There are variations of this though. Many couples prefer that the players closest to the net take the shot and some teams prefer that the player who last played the ball should play the point out.)

When you and your partner are receiving serve, remember that the key word in return of serve is "return". This word is not "slug," but just return. Even very competent players can only make one winner out of every 10, so again, don't overplay the shot.

When you are returning serve, just try to pass

the opposing net player. Once you have done this your chances of winning the point go up dramatically. Be sure to move closer to the net when you are receiving a second serve. Use mostly dink returns, occasionally go down the line, or otherwise lob to keep the poacher controlled. Use heavy drives sparingly. A dink return will force the volleyer to hit up and give you a chance to put the ball away.

When the server does not follow his serve to net, you should try to return the ball deep, take the net, and knock off any loose shots. Watch out for lobs at this stage. Hit winning overheads off short lobs, but when the lob goes deep just play a steady overhead down the middle of the court.

Don't forget, doubles is a team game. Learn to work with your partner. Communicate. Use hand signals and give verbal cues. Cover the court together, up and back or right and left.

Don't try to make all the great shots yourself. Play in such a way that your partner gets the setup and makes the winning shot.

The real fun in doubles is to view it not as an expanded game of singles, but as a game with its own unique situations.

WEATHER CONDITIONS

Now let us consider weather conditions and their effect on tennis play and tactics.

Hot Weather

Suppose it is a hot day. The first thing to realize is that the tennis ball will bounce much higher and move much faster. Heat causes the ball to come alive. Consequently, be a bit more careful about not overhitting.

Cold Weather

On a cold day, the ball will be heavy. Thus you can hit out a little more. When the ball is dead, by the way, try extra hard to hit the ball dead center, if you don't, you will get tennis elbow from the jarring off-center shots.

Windy Days

When the wind is blowing, try to think of how you can use it to your advantage. Be posi-

tive. Enjoy playing against the wind because you can hit the ball harder. When you play with the wind, exercise more care and follow your serves to the net. If it is a crosswind, attack by hitting the ball quite short to the sidelines; the wind will carry it even wider, drawing your opponent off the court. Just be careful that you don't hit wide.

As a rule, don't lob when the wind is against you. Your lob will be slowed and ready to be picked off. If you are forced to lob, hit high and deep. Conversely, if the wind is with you, take the net aggressively because your opponent's shots will be slowed for easy put-aways.

Sunny Days

Another weather condition which frustrates players is the sun. On bright sunny days, lob to your opponent when he faces the sun. When you are playing on the sunny side, close out the point quickly so you won't receive the same sun treatment you dished out.

COURT CONDITIONS

The type of surface and the condition of the court you are playing on will also affect your game tactics.

Slow Court

If you are playing on a slow court, such as clay, don't despair and say "Oh, man, I'm sunk. There goes my big serve and volley game." Instead, think of it as a chance to reach every ball. Set up well, play target tennis, direct the ball to the corners and go for a winning shot when you get a short return. Use that drop shot. Remember, on a slow court you can use more varieties of strokes because you will have more time.

Fast Court

A fast court presents a perfect opportunity for you to use your serve and volley game. Also, a slice approach down the line is particularly effective because it gives you a low bouncing ball and makes it difficult for your opponent to pass you.

Bumpy Court

Another court condition that may bother you is a bumpy one. When the ball bounce is often unpredictable, your best bet is to go to the net often and take the ball in the air.

The trick to handling all these diverse situations is to play with the right mental attitude. Try to use them to your advantage. Let the other guy worry and blame the elements for defeat.

PHYSICAL CONDITION

What about the physical condition of yourself and your opponent?

Overweight Opponent

Here is something you should know about portly people. Many who are overweight have learned how to run from side to side very economically. So if you want to tire somebody who is overweight and out of condition, running him from side to side is not likely to have the desired result. A far better tactic is to play a drop shot and a lob.

Once a player has gone to the net and chased down a drop shot and then has to run back and play a lob, and then another drop shot, the third time he hitches up his belt around his spare tire he is just about ready to quit. So the drop-shot and lob routine is an excellent tactic for someone out of condition or a bit overweight.

Gangly Opponent

Tall and gangly people reach everything. But, they cannot move efficiently to get out of the way of the ball. So hit the ball right at them. They quite often have trouble controlling close-in shots.

PLAYER CHARACTERISTICS
Lobber

To play effectively against a lobber, you must develop a good overhead. Don't crowd the net too much. Stand back a few feet in anticipation of the lob. When your opponent hits a very deep lob, be patient and just smash it back deep, and look for consistency. When you get a short lob, put the ball away decisively.

Aggressive Player

On the other side of the coin, don't hesitate to lob when you are playing a person who constantly rushes the net and crowds you. Lobbing is the best way to play an opponent who looks as if he were leaning over the net.

Two-Handed Player

There are so many two-handed players now that you ought to know how to play them effectively. The one thing you must know is that once the two-handed player is set, he will not only zing that ball, but can do so with good disguise. Because of two-handed strokers' short preparation, they can hold their shots a long time. So you must keep your shots deep against them.

And somewhat high. Two-handed players are at a disadvantage when the ball bounces high. So don't worry about hitting the ball quite high over the net when you are going for depth.

Two-handed players also have difficulty with any ball close to the body on the volley. A two-handed grip makes a backhand volley or any shot tight to the body most difficult to control. In particular, two-handed players don't like to reach for a short ball right in front of them on the two-handed side.

Arthur Ashe used this tactic successfully to win Wimbledon against Jimmy Connors. Ashe deliberately played balls short and close on Connors' two-handed backhand side. As Jimmy came forward he would shovel the ball, and Arthur would be in position to put away the weak return.

Crowding two-handed players is a good idea when they are at the net, but it is a bad idea once the ball bounces. Your best tactic then is to keep the ball wide so they have to reach for the ball.

11.

Practice Drills

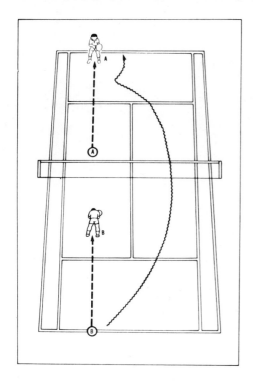 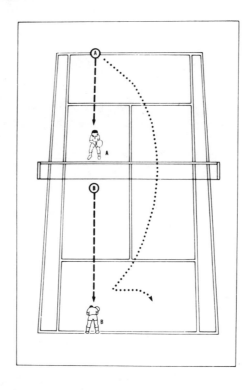

Several years ago when the indoor tennis boom was beginning, my friend Lew Gerard, a former New Zealand Davis Cup captain, invited me to Columbia, Maryland, to look at indoor tennis. I lived in California and had not been exposed to indoor facilities. Arriving at the club, I was amazed. I had never seen such a beautiful facility with high ceilings, carpeted courts, lighting, and court separating netting way up to the roofline.

Soon after my arrival some players came onto the court and started to play. It didn't look much like the tennis that we were playing in California though. One player shouted, "FBI!" And his opponent responded, "FBB!" Lew explained that they meant "first ball in" and "first ball back."

They proceeded to play the weirdest kind of hack and chop tennis I had ever seen. I asked Lew why they did not warm up and practice their strokes before starting their match.

"Oh, they would think it crazy to waste their expensive court time on practice," Lew explained.

I guess that this was the most expensive example of how not to go about playing tennis.

How Not to Play Tennis

If you don't practice, you will not improve your game. You cannot get better at tennis by playing tennis. If that sounds weird it is no less true. The reason is this. Of every hundred minutes you play tennis, about eighty minutes are wasted picking up tennis balls and changing sides. When you practice you can use your time far more efficiently.

Take lessons from your pro, who will show the correct strokes. But you must groove the stroke diligently. Schedule well-planned practice drills to develop your game. These drills should aid you in not only grooving your strokes, but simultaneously grooving your match-play capabilities.

SERVE DRILL

Perhaps the most important drill is a serve drill. It is no good standing with a bucket of balls and practicing your serve all day only to find out that once the match starts it all falls apart. To be a reliable serve, it must work when you play opponents and when you are under match play pressure.

This is how you can easily simulate match play. Play a match against Mr. Nobody. Take a bucket of balls and say to yourself, "Okay, I'm going to play one set against Nobody. If I miss my first serve, I will use my second serve. If I get the ball into the court, it is my point. If I double-fault, it is Nobody's point."

So then you play the second point. Keep score. You should win most of the points, but if you are double-faulting, you will feel silly losing to Mr. Nobody.

The purpose of the first drill is merely to get the ball into the court, thereby winning the point. As you become experienced, make the drill a bit more difficult. Allow yourself only one serve. If you miss the first, you lose the point. If you can win the match against Nobody using but one serve, you know you are improving.

When you become even better, challenge yourself still more. Mentally divide the service court into two parts, a forehand court and a backhand court. Now serve the ball once into the forehand court to win the point. For the second point, serve to the backhand side. When you get back to the forehand side again, serve to the backhand side this time.

Keep switching your target square.

When you achieve a still higher caliber of match play, divide the court into quarters and only count those serves that go into the deep quarter squares.

When you can win the serving game against Nobody 6-0, 6-0, you know you have a good serve.

RETURN-SERVE DRILL

Once your serve is under control, you need to practice your return of serve. For this you need an understanding partner.

Explain to your practice partner that you are practicing return of serve; so, please, would he ease up a little and work on serving consistently for the moment.

Practice returning the serves cross-court, practice hitting down the line. Then switch and give your partner a chance to do the same thing. Once you become consistent, both of you can increase the pace.

Practice of the serving drill and the return-serve drill should reward you with the basis of a good game.

A number of drills and on-court exercises can develop other important aspects of your game. Some are designed to improve your stroke production from the baseline. Others to improve your ability to move from side to side and forward and back from the baseline. Still others aim at creating a game situation in which you must react, move, and execute the correct shot.

Drills should be started at a rather easy pace. As the rhythm of the drill is developed, you can quicken the pace.

The following drills, used in conjunction with the serve and return-serve drills, will ensure that your game will not stagnate.

THE TEN-MINUTE WARMUP

This little ten-minute exercise is worth a hundred minutes of match play. Always start with this, whether you go out to practice or to play.

Start by hitting easy strokes on a shortened court. Make your strokes predictable. Concentrate on loosening muscles and controlling the ball.

First Minute: Forehand Volley

Play the net while your partner hits easy, controlled forehand or backhand groundstrokes to your forehand. Indicate where you want to hit your practice shots by positioning your racket as a target. Start slowly. Then add a little pace and footwork. Loosen up all the muscles involved and use the footwork for all possible volleys—high, low, right at you, a little to the side, way out to the side, and in front.

Keep one ball in play as long as you can. Have spares nearby. Don't hit hard. Concentrate on *control*.

Second Minute: Switch Roles

Now drop back and let your partner move to the net. You hit groundstrokes and he volleys forehands.

Third Minute: Backhand Volley

Same as minute one except that you hit backhand volleys at the net. Hold your racket as a target. Practice all footwork positions.

Fourth Minute: Switch Roles

You hit the groundstrokes to your partner's backhand volleys.

Fifth Minute: Alternate Forehand and Backhand Volleys

Your partner hits shots so that you can alternately play a predictable forehand or backhand volley. Your partner says out loud "forehand" and "backhand." Get the target ready before the ball arrives. Move your feet to position early.

Sixth Minute: Switch

Now you call the shots as you hit them to your partner's forehand or backhand.

Seventh Minute: Overhead Smash

Your partner lobs to you. You hit easy and controlled overheads. Your partner returns the smash if possible. The lobs should be quite deep but manageable.

Eighth Minute: Switch

You lob the ball to your partner's overheads.

Ninth Minute: Forehand Volley, Backhand Volley, Overhead

Your partner says "forehand," "backhand," and "overhead" as he directs each ball to the designated spot. Keep the rhythm going.

Tenth Minute: Final Switch

You feed the balls for forehand volleys, backhand volleys, and overheads for your partner. Now take a few warm up serves and you can start your match.

TEN-MINUTE VOLLEY DRILL WARMUP

An important drill to develop your volleying ability is this ten-minute routine.

Minute One

You and your partner stand at the net and hit *predictable* forehand volleys to each other.

Minutes Two and Three

Hit forehand volleys to your partner's backhand volleys. Switch roles for third minute.

Minutes Four and Five

Hit alternately to your partner's forehand and backhand sides. Your partner will hit only to your forehand. Reverse roles for the fifth minute.

Minutes Six and Seven

Hit to your partner's forehand and backhand. Your partner will hit only to your backhand. Reverse roles for the seventh minute.

Minutes Eight and Nine

Hit forehands to your partner's backhand. He will return the ball cross-court to your backhand. Hit the ball to his forehand, and he will hit cross-court to your forehand. Switch roles.

Minute Ten

Play random volleys.

THE VOLLEY DRILLS

These drills will develop your reflexes for match play. Not only that, you can run through these drills almost anywhere and at any time—in your backyard, or driveway. You don't necessarily need a court for this practice.

DIRECTING THE BALL

A student will complain that all his shots go cross-court, that he just can't hit down the line. Another will have the reverse problem. All of his shots go down the line and he can't hit cross-court.

Here is a simple trick that I often use to teach students how to direct the ball precisely. It is one of exaggeration.

Have a practice partner hit a ball to you and deliberately aim the ball to the left-side fence. Then aim one to the right-side fence and finally hit the ball straight forward.

Exaggerate so that you can see that you have control over the ball's direction. Then as you practice, you can become more precise in your placement.

Whenever you find that you cannot direct the ball, go back to playing a few balls in this exaggerated pattern and then work on precision again by directing the ball predictably to a target whether it is cross court or down the line.

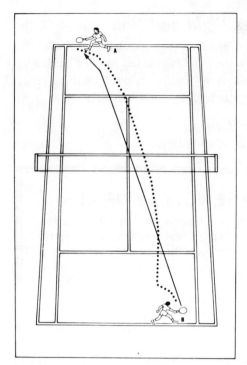

Forehand drive/cross-court drill.
Players hit forehands cross-court to each other.
Players must hit the ball on one bounce and return
balls only to the opposite forehand court area.

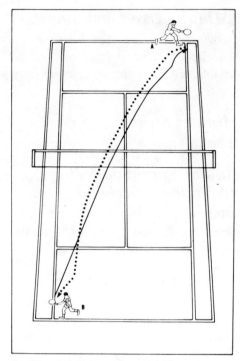

Backhand drive/cross-court drill.
Players hit backhand cross-court shots to each other.
Players must hit the ball on one bounce and return balls
only to the opposite backhand court area.

GROUNDSTROKE DRILLS

Consistent practice drills are necessary to develop your groundstrokes.

Cross-Court Forehand Drive Drill

With your practice partner in the opposite court, play forehand to forehand cross-court. You can use the entire forehand court, including the alley. Only the backhand half of the court is out of bounds.

The ball must bounce before it is hit, and as you and your partner develop control, you can add the rule that the ball must bounce only in the back half of the court—beyond the service square. Try to keep the ball in play at least ten times across the net.

Now do the same exercise on the backhand side.

Down the Line Drill

Hit forehands down the line to your practice partner. Your partner returns by hitting backhands only down the line. The alleys are good, and the ball must bounce before it is hit—no volleys allowed. You and your partner should position your feet so that you hit and return forehand to backhand shots.

Try to keep the ball in play ten times across the net, then reverse roles and positions—use the backhand side of the court to hit backhand shots down the line to your partner. He in turn returns only with forehands. Again, try to keep the ball in play ten times across the net.

Crisscross Drill

In this drill hit down the line, to your partner's backhand. He plays it cross-court. You then hit a backhand down the line to his forehand. And he plays a forehand cross-court to your forehand.

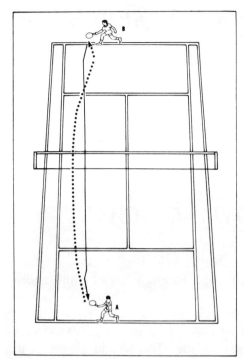
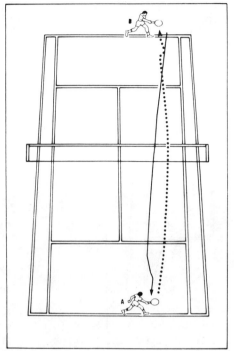

Down the Line Drill.
In the first sequence of this drill, player A hits backhands down the line to player B's forehand. In the second sequence, player A moves to his forehand alley to hit forehands down the line to B's backhand.

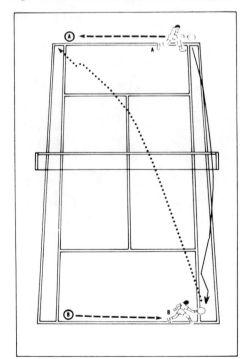
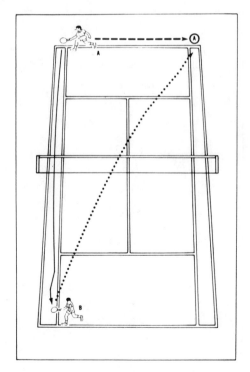

Criss Cross Drill.
Player A first hits down the line to player B who returns by hitting cross-court. Player A again hits down the line to B who hits a cross-court shot to start the pattern over again.

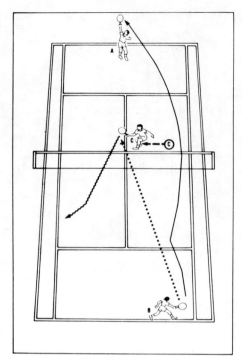

Return of Serve with Volley Drill
Player A serves to player B who returns cross-court shots. Player C at the net attempts to poach and cut off the shots.

RETURN OF SERVE WITH VOLLEY DRILL

For this drill, you'll need three players. One player serves, one player receives, and the third player volleys. The receiver returns cross-court and the net player poaches and cuts off the return. Rotate clockwise after ten sequences to give everyone a turn. When finished, do the same drill from the backhand court.

RHYTHM-OF-GAME DRILL

Here's one to help you quickly develop a sense of timing, without years of tennis experience. It is also a good introduction to poaching. You'll need three players again.

The first player is at the center of the court on the service line. The second player in the

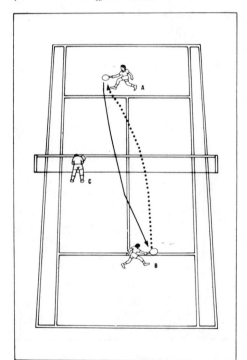

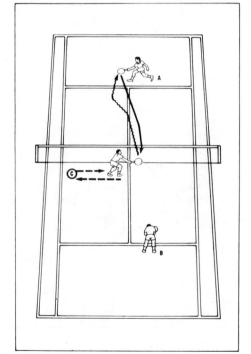

Rhythm of the Game Drill. Part I
Player A hits groundstrokes to player B. On every other hit from A, player C steps into the center of the court to volley the ball back to A.

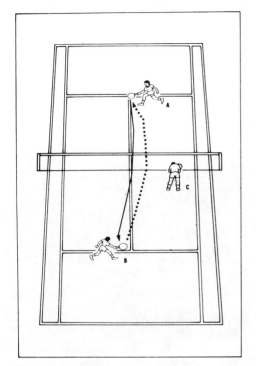 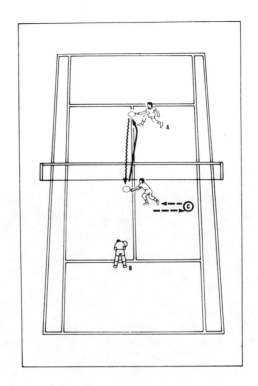

Rhythm of the Game Drill. Part II.

Same as Part I, only volleyer C moves in from the other side of the court.

opposite receiving court positions himself also at the center of the service line. The third player is up at net on the ad side.

The first player hits easy half-court groundstrokes down the center to the receiver at the opposite service line, and the receiver at the service line returns the ball. *Every other shot,* the third player who is up at net steps into the middle of the court to volley a forehand back across the net and down the center to the first player.

After you and your partners have done this for several minutes, move the volleying partner *to the opposite side,* and repeat. Now when the volleyer moves to the center of the court at every other shot, he will be returning the ball with a backhand volley. Go through this sequence for several minutes.

In the first two drills above, the volleyer returned to his position at net after each volley. Now he should step to the center, volley, and *continue across the court* to the opposite side. Skipping a shot, he should then return to the center, volley, and continue to the first corner.

The final phase in this four-phase drill is for the volleyer to cross over, stroke, continue to the opposite corner, *and return to take the next stroke as a volley,* without waiting for an intervening groundstroke exchange.

Once again, rotate positions so that all three partners receive equal time in each position. It doesn't matter whether you rotate after phase one, two, or three, as long as each of you has equal time in every position.

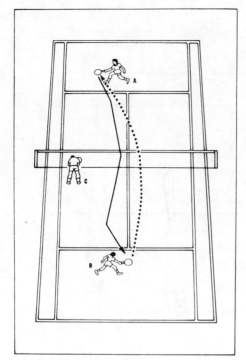

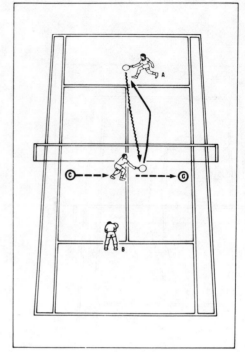

Rhythm of the Game Drill. Part III.
Same as other sequence only Volleyer C moves in from one side, hits the ball and goes
to the opposite side, waits for A and B to hit, and then moves again to
volley and return to his original position.

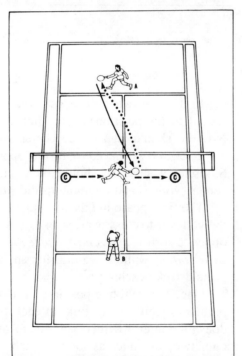

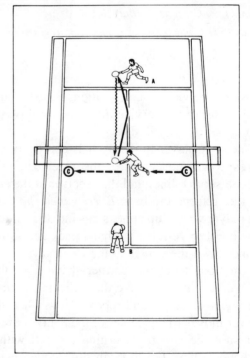

Rhythm of the Game Drill Part IV
Volleyer crosses the court, strokes and goes to the opposite side.
Then without allowing an intervening groundstroke, the volleyer returns
across the court to take the next stroke as a volley.

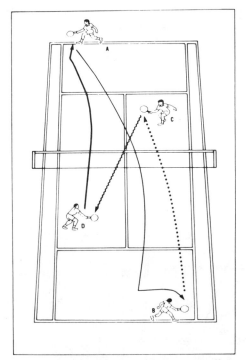

TIME-LAPSE VOLLEY DRILL

If you have a fourth partner handy, here's a variation on the rhythm-of-game drill. Set up with one player on the baseline on the court's deuce side with the second player on his baseline on the duece side. The two net players take the net positions on the ad sides of the court.

One baseliner hits a groundstroke to the other baseline player. The second baseline player returns the ball to the first volleyer, who in turn volleys cross-court to the second volleyer. The second volleyer returns the ball down the line to the first groundstroker. That sequence again: groundstroke to groundstroke, groundstroke to volley, volley to volley, volley to groundstroke.

Time Lapse Volley Drill. Four-Man Drill A.
Player A hits cross-court to player B who hits straight to player C. C then volleys his shot cross-court to player D. D hits a groundstroke to A which starts the pattern over again.

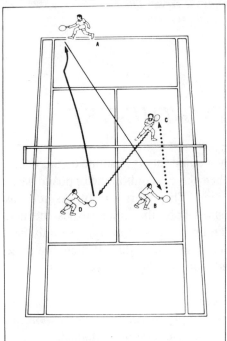

Four-Man Drill B.
Player A groundstrokes cross-court to player B at net. B volleys straight to player C who volleys cross-court to player D. D then hits his volley back to A who can then start the groundstroke-volley-volley-volley sequence again.

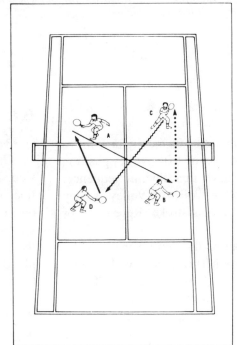

Four-Man Drill C.
Player A volleys cross-court to player B who hits straight to player C. C then volleys cross-court to player D who in turn can volley straight to A. Then the four can repeat the four-man volley-volley-volley-volley sequence again.

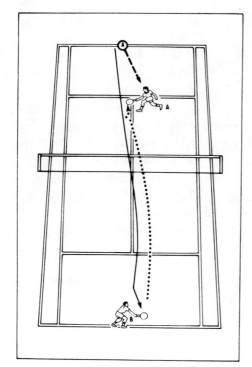 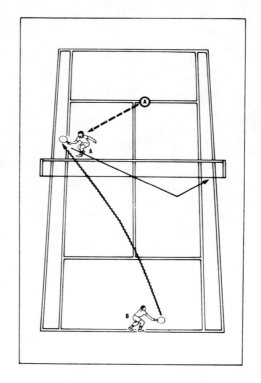

Rush the Net Drill.
Players A and B rally groundstrokes until B hits a short ball which lands inside the service line.
Player A then moves in to hit the short shot and goes on in to volley from a good net position.

Try to keep the ball in play ten or fifteen times around the circuit.

Then if you want to step up the rhythm, move the second groundstroker up to the volley position at net. Now you have this rhythm sequence: groundstroke to volley, volley to volley, volley to volley, volley to groundstroke. Repeat ten or fifteen times.

Finally, you can really step up the pace by moving the first groundstroker to a volley position. Now you have all four up at net. Try to keep the ball in play ten or fifteen times.

RUSHING-THE-NET DRILL

One player stands at his baseline on the deuce side. The other player stands at the opposite baseline on the side. They start a rally. As soon as one hits a short ball, the other rushes the net, split steps, and puts the ball away. Use only half the court, but include the alley. If there are three players, trade off so that everyone gets equal time.

All of these drills can of course be done by more players, simply by rotating one or more on or off court to give everyone a chance.

The following hot-seat drills, however, require four to be effective as they are designed primarily to raise the level of doubles play. The "hot seat," is the position played by the receiver's partner in doubles.

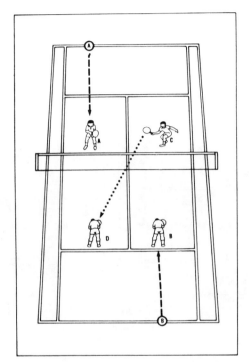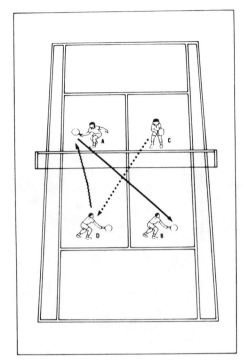

Hot Seat Drill # 1.
Player C volleys cross-court to player D. Meanwhile player A moves forward to return D's volley straight to player B who has also moved up to net for a volley.

HOT-SEAT DRILL NO. 1

The server stands halfway between the center line marker and the doubles sideline. His partner stands at the net.

The receiver is on the forehand side of his court to return the serve, and his partner (the hot-seat player) stands near the center line and the service line, thus cutting off the volley angle of the server's net playing partner.

Start the drill with the server serving an imaginary ball and rushing net. The receiver likewise returns the imaginary serve to the net man

and approaches the net. Meanwhile, the server's partner actually starts the ball in play by volleying to the hot seat player.

The hot-seat player returns the ball to the server, who is in a position to volley to the receiver, who is also now in a volleying position.

The four players exchange shots until a mistake is made. Repeat from the same positions three or four times, then rotate, so that all have a chance to work each position.

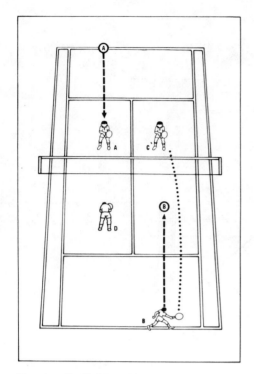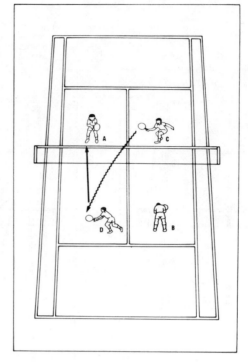

Hot Seat Drill #2.
Player B groundstrokes to player C and then moves up to the net. C volleys
cross-court to player D who is in the "hot seat." As A moves up to the net,
D volleys the ball to A. A volleys to B. Then the players play the ball out.

HOT-SEAT DRILL NO. 2

Begin from the same positions used in drill one. Again the server serves an imaginary ball and rushes the net. This time, the receiver groundstrokes to the forehand volley side of the server's partner and runs toward the net. The volleyer hits to the hot-seat player. The hot-seat player volleys the ball to the server. The server volleys back to the receiver, who may direct the ball to either player. The drill continues until a mistake is made.

When four or five shots have been made successfully in this sequence, rotate positions.

HOT-SEAT DRILL NO. 3

Start again from the positions used in drill one. This time the server serves to the receiver's forehand and follows his serve to the net. The receiver returns the ball to the server's partner, and follows his return to the net. The server's partner volleys easily to the hot-seat player, and the hot-seat player volleys to the server, who has moved to a volley position. The server volleys to the receiver, and the ball continues in play until a mistake is made. Repeat five or six times, then rotate players.

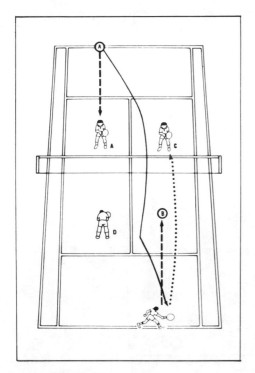
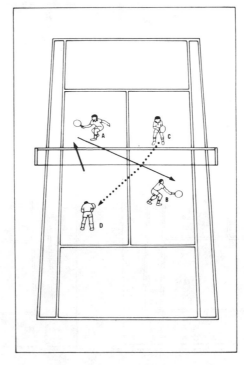

Hot Seat Drill #3.
Player A serves to player B and then follows his serve to the net. B hits to player C
and goes to the net. C cross-court volleys to player D who then volleys to A.

HOT-SEAT DRILLS ON THE ADVANTAGE POINT SIDE

All of the above drills may be done on the advantage side *except* that in drills two and three the receiver should direct his first shot to the backhand of the net player.

LOB AND VOLLEY DRILL

Take the net with your practice partner at his baseline. Your partner hits you a forehand volley and you return to his forehand. Then your partner hits you a lob that you must retrieve. While you go back to retrieve the lob, your partner comes to the net.

Feed him a forehand volley. Which he returns as a forehand. Lob over his head. While he runs back to retrieve the lob, you take the net.

Variations

You can feed backhand volleys and lobs in sequence. You can make it a three-shot drill by feeding the net man a volley, an overhead, and then a lob before advancing to the net for your turn.

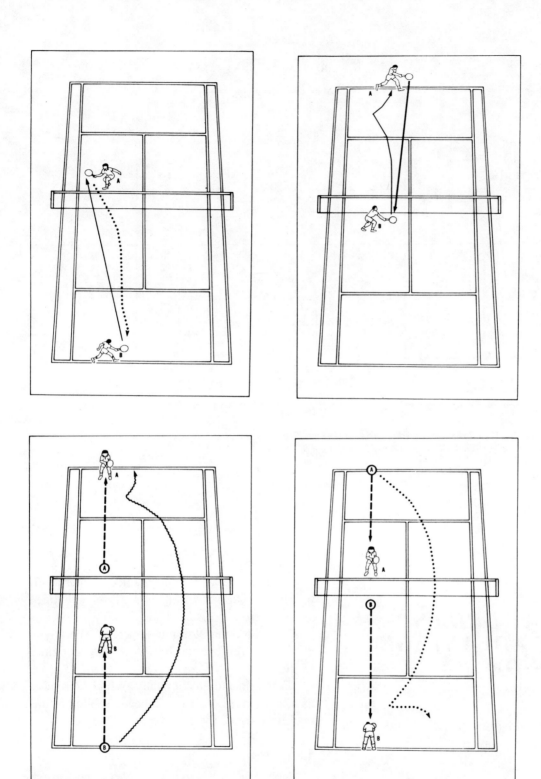

Lob and Volley Drill.
Player B hits a ball to the net man, player A. A volleys the ball back to B who lobs the ball over A's head and rushes the net. A runs the ball down and hits a drive to B. B volleys the ball back to A who lobs the ball and rushes the net while B runs the ball down.

12.

Backboard as a Practice Aid

Of all the teaching aids available, one of the oldest teaching aids in existence is the backboard. More champions have developed their initial playing skills against the backboard than by any other method known.

Backboards are everywhere. Garage doors. Gymnasium walls at schools. Basement walls. Loading docks at supermarkets. I even know of a Continental Airlines stewardess who uses a lightweight spongeball and practices her volley on the partition between the first-class and coach sections of a DC-10 during layovers.

Practice backboards, made out of nylon, are available. Among these is a Don Budge rebound net which sells for about $50. The added benefit of this model is that it is quiet—you won't disturb the neighbors when you practice early in the morning. Also, the net's rebound can be controlled, so you don't need much space to use it.

Use the backboard properly. If you slug the ball, you will learn how to play badly well. Curb your immediate impatience and practice in a controlled situation.

PRACTICE CONTROL

Stand about two or three yards from the wall. Hold the racket in front of you, and with *no* backswing tap the ball gently back and forth until you can control the ball in front of your body. Hit the ball early enough so as never to let the ball get caught behind you. Practice this on the forehand side, and then switch grips and do the same on the backhand side.

Then go from side to side, changing grips all the time. Once you can keep the ball going consistently, walk back thirteen steps (if you have that much room). You will then be at the distance from the baseline to the net. Draw a line at this position and stand about a yard behind this line.

Practice your forehand drives. Make your shoulder turn. Adjust your feet. Step forward with the left foot. Hit the ball. And follow through. Catch the ball and repeat the routine. (By the way, let the ball bounce twice when coming back to you.) Once you have some control, start rallying.

GROUNDSTROKES

Turn your shoulder, take your racket back and down, adjust your feet, hit the ball, and follow through. Let the ball rebound off the wall and bounce twice before you hit the next one. Develop a rhythm with a *two-bounce return*.

Do the same exercise on the backhand. First drop the ball, hit it, and catch it. Then let the ball come back to you with two bounces and hit it to rally. Hitting on the second bounce allows enough time to get ready so that you will not feel rushed. You will also have enough time to complete the follow-through before the next ball.

VOLLEY

Get close to the wall. Hold the racket out in front and volley the ball quite high. As you become more skillful, aim lower. Add the backhand. Once you can volley with both the backhand and the forehand, alternate the strokes against the backboard. Start high and gradually aim the ball lower as you gain control.

HALF VOLLEY

You may also practice your half volleys on the backboard. Just as the ball hits the ground, play it back gently with half volleys on both the forehand and the backhand sides.

Practicing the volley at the backboard on the forehand and backhand sides.

OVERHEAD

Backboard practice can also fine-tune your overhead smash. To set up the ball, hit the ball into the ground in front of you. As the ball ricochets off the ground, against the wall, and up into the air, you can get ready to hit your overhead smash. The harder you hit the ground, the higher the rebound for your overhead.

LOB

Using the same ball feed, practice running down balls that go over your head. After hitting the ball into the ground, let the ball go over your head. Turn around, and run down the lob. This exercise will give you confidence that you are able to run down balls that have been lobbed over you.

SERVE

The next stroke to practice on the backboard is the serve. Draw on your backboard a circle that is about three feet six inches above the ground. From your baseline serve the ball toward your circle. This way you can pinpoint your accuracy for your serve and gain confidence in your ability to direct the ball.

APPROACH SHOT

Another stroke for your backboard repertoire is to practice your approach shot. Hit the approach shot off one bounce from the backboard; go in behind the ball and finish with a volley.

Playing against the backboard can be lots of fun. You can develop a whole routine—start off and serve the ball. . .play a forehand drive with

Practicing the overhead at the backboard by hitting the ball into the ground so that it will ricochet off the wall and create a lob.

Practicing the serve against the backboard.

the ball bouncing twice. . .play a backhand drive with the ball bouncing twice. . .play an approach with the ball bouncing once. . .move in and play a forehand volley. . .as you move in, play a backhand volley. . .then a forehand volley. . .hit the ball against the ground and let the ball go over your head so you can run it down. . .return the ball. . .then hit it against the ground again. . .but this time jump up and hit an overhead smash. Fifteen-love.

What better way to have fun while developing your strokes!

13.

Physical Conditioning

Physical conditioning is something most of us read and talk about, but few of us do much about.

I envy people who are in super physical shape. By the same token, I feel sorry for those people who are in horrible physical shape.

How do you maintain a reasonable degree of physical conditioning?

Some people tell me, ''Oh, I play tennis.''

They are in for a surprise. There is no way that you can stay in shape by playing tennis. You have to do something extra to keep your body flexible and strong. Here's an example. Try it now.

Put your right hand over your right shoulder and reach toward the middle of your back. Put your left hand underneath your left armpit and reach up your back to your right hand. Your hands should interlock quite easily.

Now switch. Put your right arm underneath your armpit and your left arm over your left shoulder to interlock. Are you surprised? Many of you have discovered that your range of flexibility has diminished. But don't be downcast.

Shoulder Roll and stretch

You who flunked the test can regain your lost flexibility.

Just take any kind of rope, about two feet long, and put some knots in it. Under a hot shower, pull on the rope behind your back and try to work your way up the rope one notch at a time. Do this daily. Your range of flexibility will increase.

This easy test of flexibility is but one means of demonstrating your need for regular exercise. Tennis alone will not satisfy that need. So maintain a daily regimen of physical conditioning, whether you're one just learning the game or a professional.

Tennis players should concentrate on warmup exercises that will increase their limberness, in-crease their quickness of foot, strengthen their leg muscles, and condition their cardiovascular system.

Here are some exercises that I have used for conditioning for tennis. You may have a few of your own to add, or to substitute. The most important point about these or any other exercises is that you do them regularly.

SHOULDER ROLL AND STRETCH

Stand with your feet planted firmly and comfortably apart. Extend your arms horizontally, to the side, and rotate them alternately, as a swimmer would in a freestyle manner. Make sure you can feel the rotation of the arms in your shoulder joints and the motion of the shoulder blades in your upper back. This is good preparation for the serve. Now, reach down *slowly* and *try* to touch your left foot with your right hand. Rotate your arms again, then reach *slowly* and *try* to touch the right foot with the left hand. Stretch gradually—don't bounce. Continue rotating and reaching until you can reach your feet. This will help stretch the upper back and thigh muscles.

DOUBLE ARM ROLL AND STRETCH

With your feet planted firmly apart, roll both arms forward, then backward to loosen further your shoulder muscles for the serve. Now, *with both hands*, slowly try to touch the ground in front of you. This will stretch the lower back, and the hamstring muscles in the legs. Finally, arch back to offset the stretch of the back muscles.

ONE-FOOT HOP

Bounce up and down, first on one foot, then on the other. This will strengthen the leg muscles, especially the calf muscle. If you're a right-handed server, give your left leg a few extra bounces; if you're a lefthanded server, give your right leg the same treatment. Your off-racket side leg gets more of a workout, especially while serving, and this will help develop leg strength.

COTTON PICKER

Place the right foot over the left foot and

Double Arm Roll and Stretch

151

One-Foot Hop

KANGAROO JUMPS

Stand in position with your feet close together. Jump with both feet, and bring your knees up to your chest. This strengthens the legs and improves agility. It also strengthens the muscles around the heart.

SQUAT JUMPS

Kneel as though you were lacing a shoe, right leg up, left knee on the ground, and with both hands touching the ground on either side of the right foot. Now jump up in the air, switch feet, and come down with the left leg up, and the right knee on the ground. Repeat this switch ten times. This exercise strengthens the quadriceps—those large muscles in the front of the thigh. It also helps the hamstring and groin muscles.

ONE, TWO—CROSS OVER

Starting slowly, sidestep to your right two steps and then cross over with your left leg. Recover, then sidestep twice on your left, cross over with your right leg, and take off in the other direction without slowing the pace or lingering during the side shifts.

In summary, the old reliable conditioning workouts such as interval running—sprint, jog, sprint—should not be neglected. Stamina, as well as strength and agility, is important to the tennis player.

Remember, the important thing about exercises is to do them regularly, with sufficient intensity, and for a long enough duration to have an effect on your muscles. Start slowly, then gradually increase in intensity and duration. Do the whole pattern you have planned for yourself before you stop. If you find after several weeks that they have become too easy, increase the number of times you do each exercise. The final results will show on the court.

beside it. Now reach down with both hands and try to touch your right big toe, then touch the left big toe. Finally, stretch even farther and touch the heel of the left foot. Reverse your feet, reach with both hands, touch the left toe, then the right one, and finally all the way back to the right heel. This is a good one for the glutei—the muscles in your derriere.

CALF AND ACHILLES STRETCHES

Put one foot a comfortable distance in front of the other. Gradually lean forward, keeping the body upright. Bend the front knee and keep the back leg straight, gradually stretching the muscles.

The Cotton Picker

Calf and Achilles Tendon Stretch

Reflex

WARMUP FOR A MATCH

You should always warm up both your body and your strokes before you begin a match. Use a series of stretching and limbering exercises to warm up your body as a whole before you are on the court. Develop and follow a routine of stroke exercises to warm up your tennis game once you are on the court.

Briefly, for your physical warmup, stretch your achilles tendon, calf muscles, groin muscles, and shoulders, and do some quick skipping motions to loosen your body. Extend your range of motion by twisting your trunk from left to right and stretch as far as you can for about five or ten minutes.

After you have warmed up, you can start your racket warmups. Be sure that you practice serve, forehand, backhand, volley, and overhead smash. Go through your repertoire of strokes before the match starts.

Allow sufficient time to complete both phases of your warmup. You will then be feeling and thinking tennis from the very start of your match.

Kangaroo Jump

DIET

All of us are deluged daily by new diet and eating fads that will miraculously cause well-being. One day meat is in, the next day eggs are. Fish, cheese, alfalfa sprouts, lettuce, et cetera, have had their turns. I have no suggestions about what you should eat or drink, except one—moderation. If you eat too much or drink too much, your body is not going to function well. Eat a balanced meal, don't drink too much, and don't get fat.

**Dennis on diet:
DON'T GET FAT!**

Squat Jumps

14.

Mental Side of Tennis

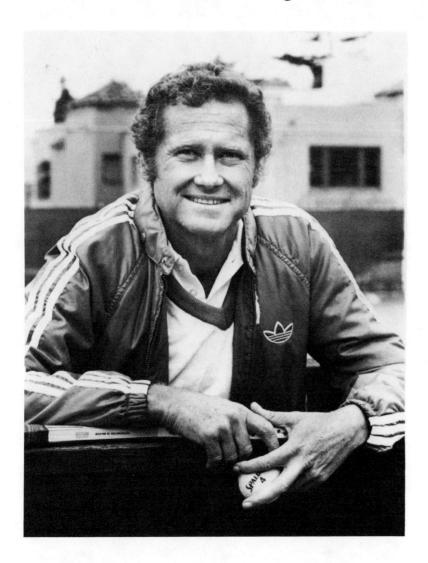

Undoubtedly, the mental side of the game is important. According to Billie Jean King, ninety percent of tennis is mental. I believe that is true once you have all the strokes.

You first need the basic equipment to play good tennis. The serve, playing the ground-strokes, the volley, the overhead smash, the lob—these are essential to a well-rounded game.

As you develop your strokes, you should at the same time develop your mental skills. You should be well motivated. You should develop your self-confidence. You should develop your concentration. You should learn to control your temper. You should practice relaxation techniques. These should all be practiced as your tennis skills are growing.

I have never talked to a tennis player who has not complained about becoming tense and losing a match because he lost concentration during the important points or when things were not going the way he expected. Every tennis player, some time or other, has been influenced adversely by mental lapses.

How can you control your emotions and make yourself play better?

PLAY THE BALL

As a young tennis player I found out that the toughest players were Australians. They always practiced just playing the ball. They learned not to worry about individual opponents with rankings or titles but just to play the ball.

Often as a youngster, I met experienced match players, well-known tournament players. Though I had been playing well and winning, I was suddenly gripped by thoughts like: "Oh, my God! I am playing this guy. He was a Wimbledon semi-finalist. I can't beat him!" And I couldn't.

If as a young person I had been trained to play the ball, I would not have been concerned with my opponent or what titles he may have won. I most

probably would not have choked.

So play the ball.

PLAY MENTAL TRICKS WITH THE SCORE

Another way to stay relaxed is mentally to fiddle around with the score. For instance, when you are ahead five-three, thirty-love, you may suddenly become tense because you are on the brink of winning. But instead of winning, you become hesitant and don't hit the ball. You lose one point, then another, then the match.

Why not mentally turn the score around. If you tell yourself that you are down three-five, love-thirty, you will probably bear down a little and win the next game. In your own mind it may now be four-five, but in fact you have just won the set.

PLAY TARGET TENNIS

Another method of mental conditioning and mind control is to play target tennis. Forget about playing your opponent or the ball. Set up a sequence of targets you want to hit. Then hit the ball to one target, and to another, and to still another, regardless of what your opponent is doing.

Now occasionally your opponent will make a great shot no matter how well you hit to your targets. Well, give it to your opponent. But by playing target tennis, you will have no tension and more often than not, you will have won the point before you complete the sequence of targets.

PLAY YOUR OPPONENT AS PRACTICE PARTNER

Another trick that is sometimes successful is pretending your opponent is a practice partner. I recommend this when players get tight and lose their rhythm. Try to rally the ball ten times back and forth across the net. Concentrate only on trying to keep the ball in play for those ten shots. Hit the ball deep into your opponent's court. Quite often you will get your rhythm back in just a few minutes.

PLAY DOUBLES AS A TEAM

One important tension controller is never to become frustrated when your partner plays poorly.

There is just no way that your partner will perform better when you shrug or give him a demeaning look or sneer because he flubs the ball. In fact, berating your partner will only make things worse. He, after all, is not deliberately playing badly. If you realize that, you will exercise understanding and offer encouragement. And by your soothing tone and calm manner you will help your partner relax and play better tennis.

There has recently been much interest in various techniques of relaxation. If you want to go into the more technical aspects of the relations of brain functions, biofeedback, et cetera, there are many books on the subject that you can read.

Some of them have become popular tennis books. Don't be lulled, however, by all the psychological interpretations and blame your stroking lapses on your mental state. Your mind cannot accomplish everything for you. You are a sucker if you think that you can lie in your bed, visualize a perfect forehand drive, and then perform it the next time you play.

I may sound old-fashioned, but there is only one way to develop a good forehand, backhand, or serve. That is by learning the strokes and practicing to perfect them. If you shortcut this procedure, you can still your frustrations by saying, ''I am not frustrated anymore. I don't have a good game, but it doesn't bother me.'' At the same time, I think, however, that the preferable choice is to acquire a worthwhile skill, cultivate it, and at the same time practice all the psychological tricks to put your mind in order so that you can avoid tension and play with easy confidence, thereby making your tennis more enjoyable while trying to win.

When people say that they ''play tennis not to win, but only to enjoy the game,'' you may be sure that their statement is absolute nonsense. You play because you like to win. That is the fun of the game. But, winning is not the sole enjoyment. If you try hard, and do your best, there is still enjoyment in the small successes you have during the match.

The one thing you must do is try. If you quit trying, you are not only spoiling the game for yourself, but also stealing a victory from your opponent. A player can win only against an opponent who tries. So always play as hard as you can so that your opponent has the opportunity to win a match, not have accept a tacit default.

THE PSYCHOLOGICAL BATTLEFRONT

Why does Borg win all the big ones? Why do you always see the same players fighting it out from the quarter finals on?

When the strokes of these players are compared, those of one player seem not particularly more effective than those of another. The difference is mental toughness, and this more often than not ultimately determines the outcome of the match.

Performing at one's full potential under stress conditions requires much self-control. The tennis player who consistently performs well under pressure has acquired mental skills and stamina that are just as real and necessary as stroking a tennis ball.

The outstanding tennis player is highly skilled at controlling appropriate muscle tension levels, at concentrating and focusing skills, at controlling anger and frustration, and at maintaining a high level of self-confidence.

Proper stroke production and mental preparedness are each necessary for successful tournament play whether on the club level or the professional level.

15.

Playing Tennis as an Older Person

Tennis can be started at any age of life. The most dramatic instance of starting tennis at an advanced age that I recall was that of Sam Schwartz.

The year was 1973. I was starting a weeklong clinic at the Boar's Head Inn, Charlottesville, Va., when I met Sam. He was a spry gentleman, slim and trim, with a peppery moustache and silvery hair.

As the students started practicing serves against the back fence, I walked over to Sam and introduced myself. After chatting a bit, I asked, "Sam, how old are you?"

After looking around furtively, he replied, "Dennis, I am seventy-six years old. Please, don't tell anybody."

Then I watched him a bit more closely and looked into his eyes. He had what looked for all the world like two coke bottle bottoms in his eyes.

"My God!" I said. "What kind of lenses are those?"

"These are full-size contact lenses," Sam explained. "I just had two cornea transplants. I have been blind for thirty years. I have just got my sight back with the transplants. Now I want to learn to play tennis so that I can rally with my grandson."

And so I taught Sam how to play.

In a week's time, I taught him to serve, to play groundstrokes, and to volley. While Sam couldn't play very well, he could pop the ball back and forth across the net. Needless to say, I had great satisfaction in knowing that I could teach an old gentleman, with new sight, to enjoy tennis, and perhaps life, a little more.

The story has an interesting sidelight. As the clinic progressed that week, Sam became my hero. I was so impressed by that man that I would follow him around and imitate whatever he did. At breakfast Sam would order two poached eggs, some skim milk, and a little juice for breakfast. I would immediately change my order from scrambled eggs, sausage, and hash browns to duplicate Sam's order.

At lunch I would lustily order a gigantic hero sandwich with mayonnaise and the works. Then I'd spy Sam sitting there with his neat little helping of cottage cheese and fruit. Quickly, I would tell the waitress to cancel my first order and bring me the same lunch as Sam.

In the evening, we would sit and have a drink. I'd order a frothy beer or a scotch. Sam would order white wine with bottled water. Again I'd have the waitress hold the first order and bring me some watered-down wine too.

Sam also ate moderately at dinnertime.

I watched him like a hawk and did exactly what he did. Talking to him about his life, I inquired about his secrets for such obviously good health.

The septuagenarian replied, "Moderation. Moderation in all things is the answer."

With that I decided I would become very moderate. Just like Sam.

At the end of the week, we were all packed and ready to leave the inn. Sam and I waited together in the front lobby. I was catching a limousine, and Sam said he had a ride.

At that moment a gorgeous young blonde, driving a Mercedes convertible, turned up the driveway and stopped in front of us.

"Dennis," Sam said, "I would like you to meet my new wife!"

I just knew there was more to Sam than eating all those stupid poached eggs every day.

How does an older person get started in tennis? Anybody, any age, can get started. Just be sure the aspirations are realistic.

Realistic aspirations for Sam were to pop the

ball back and forth in the court a few times. He wanted to know how to serve a ball, return a serve, and make a volley—all on a relatively limited scale.

For someone with poor eyesight, playing good tennis may be merely gently volleying a few balls at the net.

Each person, with his own physical capabilities and limitations, must reasonably determine for himself what his level of tennis will be. Tennis need not be a fast-moving game. A small court game of gently rallying the ball can be a very good beginning. So start slowly, and with reasonable goals. Only gradually expand them. That way, tennis will be satisfying, no matter what age you start.

Important for you as an older player is overcoming the temptation to use jab shots. Discipline yourself to use reasonably sound strokes. Don't take shortcuts.

Take lessons from a good professional. He or she will provide the instruction and reminders you need to keep your tennis game growing. With lessons and good practice sessions, you will build your game on a sound foundation.

This sound foundation will ensure two things. First, your chance of injury will be reduced, because you will be using your muscles properly. Second, a sound foundation will ensure that your level of skill will be higher than you had imag-. ined.

One of the nicest things about learning tennis as an older person is looking forward to improving. As you take your lessons and practice, you are bound to improve.

In contrast, the good players today, who started young, can now only look forward to playing a bit worse each year. For example, Jimmy Connors ten years from now will not be nearly as good as he is now. And thirty years from now, he will be a dodderer compared to what he is now.

But if you are a beginner at forty or fifty years old, and if you keep working on your game, by the time that you are sixty, you will be playing pretty darned good tennis. At seventy you will be playing really well. And when you are seventy-six, perhaps you, like my friend Sam, will have a special "inspiration."

Some adults pick up tennis after a ten- or even twenty-year layoff. Once professional careers are established or babies are off to school, many former players suddenly discover that they have gotten fat! The answer of course is to pick up that tennis racket again.

These players remember how quick and fast they were in their youth so they try to dash around as in days gone by. And that can be dangerous. An overweight, out-of-condition person should resume any physical activity carefully.

Don't rush back into the game. Start slowly and easily. Establish a schedule to get yourself back into condition. Rally and rally and rally to build up your game and your stamina. Develop your flagged muscular strength. Give the heart muscles a chance to rebuild. Give yourself time. If you rush, you will injure your arm and leg muscles at the least, and heart muscles at the worst.

If you are a former player returning to the game, scotch your dreams of winning Wimbledon. Be realistic about yourself and your present capabilities. Gradually get yourself back into shape. Work with a pro and spend some time practicing your strokes. Eventually you will regain some of your strength and skill, and achieve a solid game. Very likely, you will not only find the old groove, but discover you enjoy the game more than ever.

16.

How to Teach Your Child to Play Tennis

Vividly do I recall a parent of a nine-year-old girl I was teaching in California some years back. The girl was playing pretty well. Her father, a middle-aged man, approached me at the end of a lesson one day and announced, "We are not going to play in the under-tens next week."

"Who we, Paleface?" I asked. "I don't think that you qualify. You must be at least forty years old."

Undaunted, the father continued, "No. No. We are not going to play. . . .Ah, that is, Jeannie is not going to play."

"Well, now you have it right. Jeannie is not going to play. *She* is not going to play. Not *we* are not going to play."

This same individual, Jeannie's father, later revealed over and over how involved he was in his daughter's successes and failures on the court. When she served a ball in a match, he would involuntarily twitch. He was living vicariously. When she won, he won. When she lost, he lost. Not only did he lose, but she naturally was responsible for his losing. According to the father, "Jeannie just did not want us to win today."

Kids are not dumb. They know whether an adult has their interests and development in mind when he encourages them to play tennis, or whether he is doing it for his own ego satisfaction.

Be honest with yourself. Why are you encouraging your son or daughter to play the game? Do you want your child to achieve a degree of competence and confidence in a sport for his sake, so that he can enjoy friendly, social competition with its wins, losses, and experiences? Or do you want your child to progress in tennis so that you can bask in the glory? "Oh, are *you* the mother of that fabulous young player?"

If the latter motivates you, then you may want to join some of those unpleasant and misguided mothers and fathers on the tournament circuit. Fight with the umpires. Fight with the tournament officials. Be pushy.

If, however, you are encouraging your child to become a good tennis player for his own good and the love of the game, you will be doing him a tremendous favor. To acquire some competence at tennis is worthwhile. If your child is good enough to be selected for a high school or college team, so much the better. To play on the tournament level requires that a youngster develop a high level of skill. And, of course, very few progress to the national circuit level of tennis play and fewer still to the international level.

Whatever the future may hold for your child's tennis development, initially just encourage your child to play tennis as an enjoyable recreational sport. Play with him. Make it an outing of fun for family and friends.

Then if your youngster does seem to have an aptitude for the game, pursue developing his tennis game as he grows older.

At what age can you start? Your youngster can be one or two years old and have fun pushing and rolling a large ball around. As the child grows stronger, he will automatically start batting and grabbing out at the rolling ball. Encourage him both to grab and to block the ball.

Add a bouncing ball to your game with your child. Bounce it back and forth between the two of you. You bounce the ball to him so he bat or block it back to you.

When your child is four or five years old, he may be ready to start hitting a ball with a light racket. Wooden paddles are helpful. They aid in strengthening a young person's arms and also add stability to the stroke.

At the age of seven or eight, your little guy or gal can have quite a solid game.

Up to this age, you are basically helping the child develop eye and hand coordination. (By the way, you might be developing a soccer or baseball player. Leave the options open.)

All of your exercises with balls and paddles and junior rackets up to the age of nine should be fun. Nothing is more disheartening to me as a tennis teacher than to see a father, usually a huge former linebacker, take his son out to hit, and scream at the small one as he slugs the ball at him.

"Johnny, watch the ball!"

Johnny misses the ball.

"I said watch the ball!"

The father slugs another ball. Johnny misses the ball.

"You did not watch the ball. Now really

watch it this time!"

Johnny misses it again.

"Watch the ball, damn it!" Dad screams.

"I am. I am watching it. The ball just went by. It is round and yellow," cries the frustrated boy with tears streaming down his face.

At this stage the father huffs off the tennis court, muttering, "Just like his mother. . .just like his mother. . ."

How sad. The game can be such fun. Enjoy tennis with your youngster. Even when your child reaches nine, keep tennis simple and enjoyable. Rally with the young player. Hit him forehands and backhands, volleys and overheads, but keep instruction very basic.

Watch to make sure he is moving easily and directing his shots. Allow him to feel a swell of achievement and confidence when the two of you keep a ball going back and forth ten times or twenty times.

When your child starts formal lessons and starts learning the strokes of the game, help him to practice. Still go easy on the details of technique and tactics.

If your youngster develops a genuine desire to play, increase the number of practice sessions, increase the number of lessons, and help him or her to understand tactics and techniques better.

Be sensitive about pushing too hard. If you push too hard, the youngster will reject tennis altogether. Young people who have been pressed hard quit playing tennis as soon as they get away from mom and dad. That doesn't benefit anyone. So don't push too hard. Let your child find his own tennis niche with your support and guidance.

On the other hand, if you do happen to have a very talented youngster, don't forget to push. But know how hard to encourage, prompt, and drive. Correctly motivated, your child will play without tremendous pressure throughout junior life. He will play in college, as a young adult, and in the seniors.

Remember, just play pitty-pat tennis with your child up to nine. Make it fun. From age nine onward, you are dealing with developing a lifelong recreational or perhaps a tournament player. Throughout these stages, support, encourage and share your enjoyment of tennis with your children.

You be the one who is on the court and ready to rally with them when they ask. Reward them with Cokes for twenty shots across the net. I am not averse to rewarding children to get them to practice.

One of my students, we'll call her Monica, is an excellent example of the success of rewards and praise.

When I first met Monica she was an uncoordinated young girl and completely unmotivated. She didn't like tennis. She hated to run. Her then fashionable "Beehive" hairdo would get mussed.

Her mother, though, really wanted Monica to learn to play. We had to motivate her some way.

I asked, "What does Monica like?"

"Monica loves money," her mother responded without hesitation.

That decided it. Every lesson Monica completed would net her $5. Every match she played and won would bring $2. Every loss paid $1.

When Monica next came for a lesson, she could hardly wait to get on the court. When she lagged on a few shots and didn't run, the mere mention of the $5 bait brought her back into action.

In only a few months, Monica developed into a much better tennis player (and wealthy to boot). She even started to like her lessons.

One day she came to me and said, "Dennis, you just can't believe what just happened when I was standing outside the ladies locker room. I overheard the girl who is scheduled to play me in next week's tournament call me a 'tough player.' Can you imagine? She thinks that I am tough!"

While she was talking, she actually began to stand more upright and looked much more self-confident.

I am happy to add that Monica went on to become quite a fine tennis player and was ranked nationally.

So there are many different ways to motivate youngsters. Find out which applies to your child and use it.

Adults, particularly parents, experience two major problems when dealing with children, both on the tennis court and off. First, you will find it difficult to be rational with children. You can talk and explain and talk and explain, but it is like talking to a wall.

Then, like magic, one day when you have not said anything or done anything different from all those other times on the court, everything suddenly starts to go right.

Children will pull this turnaround from the other direction too, of course. All of your interest and work seem to be paying off beautifully and the young player's strokes are well timed and flawless. Then one Saturday morning, the world flipflops and the child acts as though he had never picked up a tennis ball, let alone successfully hit it with a tennis racket. So with children, anything can happen. Be patient and enjoy your time with them.

Another quirk of children that may or may not be a problem is that children are very imitative. Whatever you do, they very likely will do. What you say and what you do had better correlate.

Children's desire to imitate adult actions can be used advantageously. If you have a regular practice or warmup routine, the children will follow suit. If you rally for ten minutes before the start of each match, the children will do the same because they believe it is the adult thing to do.

If you tell them to rally for ten minutes before their matches, but you just start right off because "you are adults," you can be sure that they will not rally.

The same rule applies to court behavior. If you behave poorly on the court during a match or after a match, you will be hard put to teach your children to be calm, courteous, and good winners and losers.

Being an adult tennis player has more responsibilities than some of us realize.

17.

Mini Tennis

A game of mini tennis not only can be fun, but also can provide the fundamentals of tennis for both young and older first-timers within a short period of time.

With about thirty minutes of simple instruction, you can teach anyone to play a modified game of tennis complete with groundstrokes, serves, volleys, and even overhead smashes. Here is how.

First, simply bounce the ball on the ground and then on your racket. Keep the ball under control by hitting lightly.

Second, share the ball with a partner. Stand about six feet apart. The ball rebounds from the ground to your partner's racket, to the ground, and back to your racket. Develop a rhythm by letting the ball bounce easily to the ground between each of your hits.

Third, move onto the tennis court and gently pop the ball over the net to your partner. You

Mini Tennis—Steps One and Two: After you can each bounce the ball off your racket, bounce the ball on the ground sharing a ball with your partner.

Mini Tennis—Step Three: Finally, start to bump the ball over the net to your partner

should stand about about twelve feet apart and hit the ball with almost no backswing and very little followthrough.

In these three short steps, you have the beginning of a forehand. Most important, throughout the mini-tennis progression keep the ball under control by hitting gently and directing it carefully. As control grows, you and your partner may little by little step back from the net. As you move back, your stroke will naturally start to lengthen both in the backswing and the followthrough.

Mini Tennis: Develop a forehand volley in four quick steps.
Block the ball with your hand.
Block the ball with your racket face.
Move your hand halfway down the shaft and block the ball.
Move your hand all the way down to get the correct forehand grip and block the ball for a volley.

Mini Tennis: Develop a backhand volley in four quick steps.
Block the ball with thumb.
Block the ball with racket face.
Move your 'hand down shaft and block again.
Move your hand all the way down to get the correct backhand grip and block the ball for a volley.

Now you have a ''forehand.'' From the ''forehand'' move to the volley. To learn the forehand volley, stand at the net and simply hold your hand up to block the ball. Then hold your racket face in the palm of your hand and block the ball again. Next, grasp your racket halfway down the shaft and block another ball. Finally, move your hand all the way down the shaft and block the ball back for a forehand volley.

The backhand volley is equally simple. Again, stand at the net and block the ball on your backhand side with your thumb. Then hold the racket face in front of your thumb and block a second ball. Move halfway down the shaft and get the feel of blocking the ball on the backhand side. Finally, move your hand all the way down the handle to the correct grip position and keep a rally going.

Now you can volley! Keeping the same grip on the racket that you have developed through the backhand volley sequence, move directly to hitting the backhand. Gently tap the ball back and forth across the net on the backhand side by blocking the ball after it bounces. Stand close to the net and just block the ball back. No backswings or follow-throughs yet. Then after gently tapping the ball back and forth across the net successfully a few times, move back slowly. As you experienced with the forehand, you will naturally start to lengthen your backswing and develop a follow-through as you direct the ball farther to clear the net.

There is your backhand. Once you know your groundstrokes and the volley, all that remains is the serve to get you onto the courts and playing. Learn the serve by learning how to hit a very easy overhead smash.

Standing close to the net, bring your racket back behind your back. Reach up and stop at the height of your swing. Then have your partner

Mini Tennis: Develop an overhead smash.
Turn sideways to net and hold racket behind back.
Reach up and contact the ball.

feed you a ball. Reach up and just block it back over the net. Do not follow through. Your intent is to hit the ball gently back into the court and just practice finding the contact point.

This gives you an overhead smash.

Next comes the serve. Feed yourself overhead smashes instead of having your practice partner hit them to you. Remember, start with the racket behind your back. Release the ball easily into the air, reach up and block it over the net. Repeat your serve, gradually moving farther back as your consistency grows. You do not need a follow-through at this point to serve and start

game. So just tap it in.

Now you have a basic serve. In only a few minutes you have gone through all the strokes in mini form. You can rally forehands and backhands back and forth. You can play volleys and the overhead smash. And you can serve.

The key to this instant success method is that everything is first learned very close to the net with almost no backswing and no followthrough.

From this .control base the game can easily be expanded by moving further back on the court and allowing the strokes to grow naturally in size.

18.

Tennis Etiquette

Has this ever happened to you?

You are playing an exciting point when from the court next door an insistent voice calls, "Hey! Ball!"

Finally you are distracted enough to turn to the court next door and see the player demanding his ball, which has rolled onto your court. He does not care that you are still playing a point. You pass the ball back. Of course, old "Hey Ball" doesn't say thank you.

A bit later by chance you serve a fault first serve and your ball rolls into the next court. You serve another ball and the point is in progress when suddenly you hear, "Hey! Ball!" Startled, you miss your shot and most likely trip on the ball "Hey Ball" has thrown back onto your court.

This perhaps is an extreme example of bad tennis manners, but it illustrates my point. Players should learn the basic etiquette of the game. Don't ask for or return a ball during play.

Don't be cheap about tennis balls or miscellaneous court costs, etc.

Have an arrangement to alternate supplying the balls. Or just share the expense of the tennis balls and court time. Make your own agreements—the winner takes the balls or whatever—but don't be cheap. Pay your share.

A hint. Whenever a much better player invites you to play with him or her, bring the balls as a courtesy. You will gain the most from the match because of the additional practice you are getting. The better player may not necessarily accept that you should supply the balls, but your generous gesture will be appreciated.

Spin for sides and give your opponent the choice of calling. If he wins the toss, he chooses to serve, receive or choose a side. He also has a fourth option of insisting you choose first.

Once the game starts, don't be noisy. Don't moan or groan during every point. Don't shout and disturb everybody.

When playing doubles always consult with your partner as to who should serve first. The two of you may decide to spin for serve, but at least you have not just grabbed the balls and started serving.

Also, when you play doubles, don't contradict your partner. If he calls a ball out, it is out unless he chooses to change his call.

Be a good loser and a gracious winner. When you have finished your match, shake hands and thank your opponent for the match. If you have won, be tactful. Compliment your opponent by saying: "We played a good match. I really enjoyed it." Mention his good shots.

If you have lost, don't end the match by saying, "Oh, I played lousy." Instead, be enough of a person to say, "You played very well."

Last, and most important, don't cheat. Here are the rules of tennis. *You rule your own side.* Whatever happens on your side is your business. Nobody should interfere with that side. If you think a ball is in, it is in. If you think that a ball is out, it is out. There is no further consideration.

Never, never fall into the habit of saying that you did not see the ball so "please take two." If you can't or don't see the ball, you must call the ball good. That is all there is to it. Otherwise you could just close your eyes every time your opponent hits a giant overhead or a super shot, and say, "Oh, I didn't see it. Please take two!" Nonsense. Call the ball honestly and fairly. If you cannot see the ball, call it good.

Remember, if you are considerate on the court, you will always have an ample supply of playing partners.

THE RACKET SPIN

Should you win the racket spin, you have four, not three, choices. You may take sides, serve, receive, or let your opponent choose.

19.

Grips and Strokes

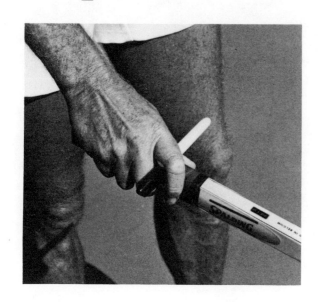

There are different grips for different strokes just as there are different strokes for different folks. The most common grips are the Western, the Continental, and the Eastern.

The Eastern grip is most commonly taught by teachers. Basically, the forehand Eastern grip is like shaking hands. The Continental grip places the hand a little bit more on top of the racket than the Eastern. The Western grip moves the hand to a position more underneath the racket.

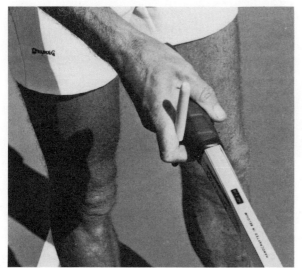

Eastern forehand

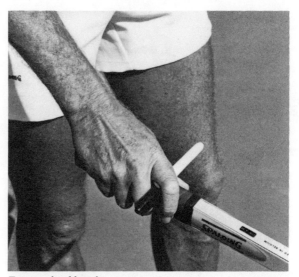

Eastern backhand

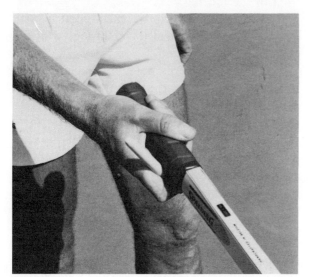

Western

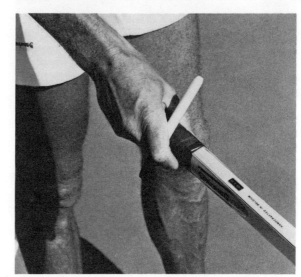

Continental or Service

Eastern grip holds the racket face on edge and brings the contact point just in front of player's left leg.

Continental grip tends to open the racket face and bring the contact point further back than the Eastern.

Western grip tends to close the racket face and is hit early, well in front of the Eastern grip's contact point.

The Eastern forehand grips place the racket face on edge with your ball contact spot just in front of the left leg.

The Continental grip's contact point is back between the left leg and the right leg, with the racket face a little open.

The Western grip's point of contact will be in front of the left foot, and the racket face will be slightly tilted toward the ground.

Another difference among grips is the angle formed between the racket and the forearm. With the Continental grip, the racket will be almost at ninety degrees up in the sky. With the Western grip, the racket will probably be at 180 degrees to your forearm. With the Eastern grip, the angle will probably be about 120 degrees.

So be careful when you decide to make a grip change because your point of contact will change and the angle of your racket face also will change.

20.

Equipment Pointers

Almost every racket made is overengineered for the player's ability. In other words, your racket is capable of hitting the ball very well, and if the ball does not go straight, the racket is not to blame.

You have a wide choice of rackets—wood, metal, fiberglass, graphite, or combinations thereof, with standard, mid-size and jumbo heads available.

My experience is that one can adjust to any kind of racket within a short period of time provided the racket is evenly balanced.

A substantial amount of shock transfers when the ball is hit. To avoid the racket twisting and to reduce the possibility of arm injury, use a grip large enough to fit your hand comfortably.

Most professional stringers recommend that the standard size racket be strung between fifty-five and sixty pounds. Less experienced players will play better with a racket strung between fifty and fifty-five pounds.

I used a standard size wooden racket all my life. I had tried the bigger rackets but could not get the hang of them. Then Spalding, my racket endorsement company, asked me to try out one of its new mid-size models. Reluctantly I agreed—reluctantly because my prior experience with oversize rackets had been disastrous. I practiced diligently for two weeks with utter frustration. I could rally but as soon as there was a tight point, I would blow it. I phoned the director of promotions for Spalding and said there was no way I could endorse that particular racket. Shortly after the phone call, a friend of mine by the name of Charlie Hoover (equipment director of Adidas, my clothing endorsement company) happened by and said, "Well, I see you finally weakened—you're playing with a mid-size!"

"No, it's a useless bloody thing," I told him. Charlie picked it up and smacked it against the strings of another racket and immediately remarked, "The tension is too low."

That same day I had my stringer re-string the racket to a higher tension—well over 60 pounds—and it was like a miracle from tennis heaven. I started playing better that same day, lifting my game by at least 10 per cent over the level it had been for the previous three years.

Since then, my entire teaching staff has switched to larger-sized rackets by choice, with similar good results. Morale: the larger heads definitely have some merits and you should explore them to see if one is for you. But definitely be sure to go with the manufacturer's recommended stringing tension, not with the tension you were used to when you played with a smaller racket.

As to the type of string, I find very little difference between good man-made strings and natural gut. Only on the highest levels of play will the qualities of natural gut be an advantage over nylon.

The fact that the man-made strings are usually impervious to water and are much cheaper than natural gut should be sufficient inducement not to spend the extra money on gut. But if playing with gut strings makes you feel good, then buy it.

You can play tennis in any type of comfortable clothing (most everyone has a pair of gym shorts and a T-shirt). However, you will need a good pair of shoes. If you are going to splurge on any one item of tennis equipment, buy yourself the best pair of shoes you can afford. Your shoes must have adequate arch support and provide good shock absorption.

21.

Epilogue

Over the twenty-five years that I have been teaching tennis, I have received thousands of letters from students who have participated in my tennis clinics and others who have somehow been exposed to my teaching.

A number of the letters are friendly thank-you notes for a good time and a good learning experience. Sometimes, though, the letters reveal that participation in the clinics has meant a great deal more.

The one perplexing bit of praise that I often receive from both experienced clinicgoers and newcomers is this: ''We were so surprised that you were actually present and did the teaching.''

Now why the devil should this be surprising? When I advertise that I will conduct a clinic, surely the student has the right to expect me to do just that. I am grateful that I have too great a respect for my profession to let my television appearances, exhibitions, or endorsement obligations conflict with my primary obligation of teaching my students.

For some people, attending a tennis clinic turns out to be much more than I or the student really expected. Surprisingly, students have written that their lives have been completely changed, that they now have new confidence in themselves, that they now have the courage to make important decisions about life. It is amazing to me that a tennis clinic can do all this, but ap-

parently it does happen.

I am pleased also by those who have written that I have inspired them to become more aware of their physical condition—inspired them to slim down, or to stop smoking, or to take greater interest in their health generally.

Other letters that please me greatly are from people who had despaired that they would never be able to play, but who now can; from students who had hitches and herky-jerky motions but who can now swing smoothly; from players who had lost to the same opponents for five years but who can now trounce them; from young players starting out on the circuit and telling me that I had given them confidence to win; from established players who have won Wimbledon because of some small correction I was able to make in their stroke production; from heads of state who thanked me for contributing to the improvement of their society through my tennis teaching.

These letters make me feel good, and I was tempted to share some of them with you but I thought that maybe you would misunderstand and assume that I was just being self-serving. Instead, I think you will find it interesting to read an analysis of my teaching by a sports psychologist, Dr. Jim Loehr. This study appeared in *International Tennis Weekly,* the official newspaper of the Association of Tennis Professionals.

A Psychologist's View of the Dennis Van der Meer Standard Teaching System

by Dr. James Loehr
American Psychological Association

As a practicing sports psychologist and tennis player, I've been aware of many tennis teaching programs and clinics that have come along, only to fall by the wayside in a short time. Surely, they all had something worthwhile, something beneficial to offer. Obviously, it wasn't enough, or wasn't offered in the right way, or their success would have been of longer duration. One program, however, seems to have withstood the test of time. It continues to grow and its worldwide popularity is undeniable.

Why has the Dennis Van der Meer Teaching System been so uniquely successful over the years? Why has this particular approach continued to prosper when others have come and gone? With enthusiastic supporters such as Billie Jean King, Margaret Court, Juan Gisbert, Francois Savy, Manalo Santana, as well as literally thousands of teaching pros from around the world, the Van der Meer System must obviously get results.

My question, from a psychologist's point of view, was *why?* Why does this system get results—and how does it accomplish this? Could it be linked solely to the charisma of its leader? Or is it the result of a highly effective learning and teaching model?

It seemed to me that the only satisfactory way to answer that question was to take a week of my time and experience the program from the inside.

Instead of attending the regular clinic for players, I selected the Van der Meer program which is designed for teaching pros and extends over an eight-day period. After just a few days, the answer to my question became obvious. Dennis Van der Meer has developed a systematic teaching and learning system that only a learning psychologist could fully appreciate. To express clearly my observations, I would like to discuss the Van der Meer System as it relates to a number of widely accepted psychological learning principles and practices.

Establishing the Proper Learning Climate—Firm yet Friendly. From the very beginning, Dennis and his staff established an atmosphere that I would describe as serious, yet, at the same time, very friendly and personal. Within the first thirty minutes, *all* of the staff knew every one of the forty-two students by name. I traced two individuals through their activities during the morning of the first day and, during a one-hour period, their names were spoken an average of thirty-two times each. All of the staff was obviously trying to help every participant feel relaxed, comfortable, and involved. Dennis's frequent interjection of humor served to further enhance this atmosphere.

Although each participant was quickly made aware of where and how his or her strokes differed from that which was considered optimal and classically sound, the corrective action was taken in a climate that was unmistakably positive and supportive. Clearly, Dennis has made a genuine effort to select carefully staff members who are positive people and who possess a sort of contagious enthusiasm.

Consistent Use of a Clearly Defined Learning Model. The Van der Meer System rests firmly on the premise that learning proceeds from the simple to the complex. Every stroke has been broken down into its most fundamental building blocks. All participants, regardless of their skill and own individual strokes, are carefully guided through each phase of the learning progression. Mastery of each level is required before progressing to the next, more complex level.

Learning by Doing. Dennis Van der Meer most certainly understands the importance of this principle. A brief discussion of the concept, a demonstration, and then the participant immediately begins *doing* the routine. Every concept, demonstration, and progression is quickly followed by everyone physically performing the sequence.

Consistent and Immediate Feedback. There is little chance for error, as all participants are given immediate feedback as they practice. Every instructor has been trained to detect deviations from the standard model. One point that was very surprising and significant to me was that the feedback given to the students was consistent throughout all the staff. This virtually eliminated the confusion that commonly arises out of conflicting staff direction and suggestions.

Effective Use of Positive Reinforcement. Corrective measures are taken within a predominantly positive framework. All instructors have been trained to accentuate the positive while, at the same time, requiring careful student adherence to the desired model. The staff, and particularly Dennis, represent very potent reinforcers. All staff members are constantly reinforcing with

comments like, "That's it, Sandi—looks good," "Now you're getting it, Bill—let's keep repeating it," or "All right, Mary—now move on to the next progression."

Steady Diet of Success. Student failures are minimized by working from the simple to the complex. Everyone, regardless of personal skill level or stroke mechanics, experiences consistent success. Divergence of skills or strokes presents no particular problem within the system. The learning system is actually structured to protect the less skillful learner from embarrassment and failure.

Staff Members Model What They Teach. The participants are not asked to learn something that the staff hasn't already clearly modeled. The adage "Do as I say—not as I do" is definitely not applicable here. Obviously, much time and effort have been set aside to achieve this kind of internal consistency, and the overall effect is very powerful.

Effective Use of Visual Feedback. Video replay is immediately provided for each participant before any corrective procedures begin, and immediately following. Each participant can clearly "see" any positive change and where additional work may need to be done. Also, prior to any corrective procedures, Dennis models the particular stroke being reviewed to give each person a mental image of what the stroke should look like. "This is what it should look like—and this is what you look like." This kind of modeling process can further help the student get a clearer mental picture of how the individual parts relate to the whole of the stroke.

Highly Organized yet Flexible Routine. Although a definite schedule of events was presented, whenever Dennis sensed that the group was tiring, their concentration lagging, or that the routine was beginning to suffer in the sun and heat, a sudden change would be introduced. He was acutely sensitive to the tempo and mood of the group, and as a result, students remained tuned in to the learning process.

A good example of the flexibility of the program and staff occurred on the third day of the clinic when a sudden thunderstorm drenched the courts. All forty-two pros and ten staff members simply moved inside to a relatively small gymnasium, and continued the program very effectively until the courts dried, with only minor alterations. This was a rather impressive demonstration to the teaching pros of what could be done if things didn't work out exactly as you planned them.

Perfect Practice Makes Perfect. Structured practice within a well-defined framework is encouraged. Every effort is made to get participants to practice correctly. Practice for the sake of practice is discouraged. Perfect practice is the goal.

Unique Corrective Procedure. Participating pros are not allowed to hit balls full speed during the learning routines. This restriction forces a sort of slow-motion learning system which I found most intriguing.

Everyone was capable of executing a perfect stroke at reduced speeds. Put in learning theory terms, the stimulus was introduced at a low enough level so as to not evoke prior learning responses.

Those participants who were muscling or forcing the stroke began to experience a relaxed feeling for the new strokes.

This slow-motion technique provides a framework whereby the purely automatic responses of the student can be subjected to careful analysis and changed where necessary.

The Process of Reconstruction—Only One Mistake at a Time. Nothing can be more discouraging to someone than to have four or five problem areas identified simultaneously. All videotape analysis, stroke-production reviews, and corrective actions are limited to only one specific area at a time. A deliberate attempt is made by the staff not to overwhelm the participant with a barrage of problem areas. Dennis's philosophy is: "Keep it simple, keep it specific, and one thing at a time."

Relevance and Practicability. A genuine attempt was made to relate each phase of the clinic experience to the real-life practical problems of the teaching tennis professional. Anchoring the experiences and learning to real-life problems and situations made the entire experience more meaningful.

The TennisUniversity program takes the teaching pros and makes them students again, gets them to reexperience the feelings of being a learner again, of being taught rather than being a teacher. From this vantage point, a host of new insights can be realized. Pros sometimes have flaws in their games—just like their students. According to Dennis, the best way to understand the system and to believe in it is to apply it to yourself. To intensify further the feelings of being a learner, the pros are required at times to learn strokes, progressions, etc., with their non-dominant hand; for example, if they were right-handed, they had to use their left hand.

It might be of interest to note that a Van der Meer tennis clinic for juniors happened to overlap part of the University program, affording me an opportunity to compare the two programs. I was pleasantly surprised to find the two nearly identical except for the emphasis on teaching in the University program. The overall design, corrective routines, and basic learning model were identical.

In summary, Van der Meer's Tennis-University represents a teaching and learning system that rests firmly on a number of well-established psychological learning principles. It is a system that is consistent with sound principles of learning and the results have given it longevity. ■

I hope that
some time, somewhere,
I will have the pleasure
of your company
in one of my clinics.
Drop me a line.

My address is:
Dennis Van der Meer
Box 4739
Hilton Head Island
South Carolina   29928
U.S.A.